UNDERSTANDING THE REVELATION
MICHAEL SCANTLEBURY

UNDERSTANDING THE REVELATION: AN IN-DEPTH STUDY
Copyright © 2023 by Michael Scantlebury

Editorial Consultant: Anita Thompson – 604-521-6042

All rights reserved. Neither this publication nor any part of this publication may be reproduced or transmitted in any form or by any means, electronic or mechanical, including photocopying, recording or any information storage and retrieval system, without permission in writing from the author.

All Scripture quotations, unless otherwise indicated, are taken from the Revised Standard Version. Copyright © 1946, 1952, and 1971 the Division of Christian Education of the National Council of the Churches of Christ in the United States of America. Used by permission. All rights reserved. All Scriptures marked KJV are taken from the King James Version; all marked NIV are from The New International Version; and those marked MSG are from The Message Bible and is used by permission.

Hebrew and Greek definitions are from James Strong, Strong's Exhaustive Concordance of the Bible (Peabody, MA: Hendrickson Publishers, n.d.).

Michael Scantlebury has taken author's prerogative in capitalizing certain words that are not usually capitalized according to standard grammatical practice. Also, please note that the name satan and related names are not capitalized as we choose not to acknowledge him, even to the point of disregarding standard grammatical practice.

ISBN: 978-1-4866-2356-3
eBook ISBN: 978-1-4866-2357-0

Word Alive Press
119 De Baets Street Winnipeg, MB R2J 3R9
www.wordalivepress.ca

Cataloguing in Publication information is can be obtained from Library and Archives Canada.

BOOKS BY MICHAEL SCANTLEBURY

Are We Living in the End-Times or Last Days?
Heaven and Earth – A Biblical Understanding
Understanding the Kingdom of God and The Church of Jesus Christ
Eschatology – A Biblical View
As It Was in the Beginning, So Shall It Be…
Daniel In Babylon – The Study Guide
Principles for Victorious Living Volume II
Principles for Victorious Living Volume I
Present Truth Lifestyle – Daniel In Babylon
Esther: Present Truth Church
The Fortress Church
Called to be An Apostle – An Autobiography
Leaven Revealed
Five Pillars of The Apostolic
Apostolic Purity
Apostolic Reformation
Jesus Christ The Apostle and High Priest of Our Profession
Kingdom Advancing Prayer Volume I
Kingdom Advancing Prayer Volume II
Kingdom Advancing Prayer Volume III
Internal Reformation
God's Nature Expressed Through His Names
"I Will Build My Church." – Jesus Christ
Identifying and Defeating the Jezebel Spirit

Contents

Foreword	VII
Introduction	IX
Chapter One **Dating the Revelation**	1
Chapter Two **Breakdown of The Revelation**	13
Chapter Three **A Deeper Look into the Messages to the Seven Churches - I**	19
Chapter Four **Gnosticism**	41
Chapter Five **A Deeper Look into the Messages to the Seven Churches - II**	45
Chapter Six **The Seven Seals**	59

CHAPTER SEVEN
THE MARK OF THE BEAST AND THE SEAL OF GOD   81

CHAPTER EIGHT
SEVEN LAST PLAGUES   95

CHAPTER NINE
THE FALSE BRIDE   107

CHAPTER TEN
MARRIAGE OF THE LAMB   111

CHAPTER ELEVEN
THE THOUSAND YEAR   115

CHAPTER TWELVE
THE NEW HEAVENS AND NEW EARTH   127

CHAPTER THIRTEEN
CLOSING THE REVELATION   137

OTHER EXCITING TITLES
BY MICHAEL SCANTLEBURY   147

Foreword

If there is one book in the Word of God that needs more clarification, understanding, and direction, it is the book of Revelation. Filled with symbols, images, and narratives that boggle the imagination, this book, placed at the very end of the Bible, bears a record of the testimony of Jesus Christ and the things He saw. Anyone who reads and hears the words of this profound book of the Revelation will be blessed.

Despite the mystery surrounding Revelation, you should aim to read it with an open heart and mind. Apostle Michael Scantlebury, an expert at articulating God's ideas for planet Earth as well as a prolific writer, seriously undertakes his writing assignments as a call of God from his Heavenly Father to bring clarity and correct interpretation of Scripture to fellow Believers, and this book is no exception. His gift reveals understanding, wisdom, and instruction of God's Kingdom by introducing truth that will leave you living on a higher cognitive and spiritual level.

In "**Understanding the Revelation**," an in-depth study of the book of Revelation, Apostle Scantlebury opens the Believer's minds to truths and understanding that the reader might not have realized or understood otherwise. Apostle Scantlebury starts each journey of his work step by step, verse by verse, and chapter by chapter all to methodically unveil to the reader truths that will cause them to ponder, think, investigate, and ultimately decide on whether to believe old and antiquated theories and hypotheses presented since the beginning of Christendom or to embrace the present truth as it is researched in great depth as well as concisely and accurately presented.

As I digested this captivating book, the author had me riveted with attention, piqued with curiosity, and at times spiritually emboldened and enlightened as I weighed, pondered, questioned, and collected what was presented into organized thoughts I could eventually understand and articulate myself for the benefit of others.

In this book **"Understanding the Revelation,"** and in his many other books I have read, Apostle Scantlebury heavily researched, dissected, and aligned with other noted men and women of God who are on the same path of unveiling the truth where it is – not where one might assume it was from hearing the same thing repeatedly throughout our lives. It is a prayerful work by a man who seeks after the heart of God for the elevation and empowerment of the Body of Christ.

Apostle Michael Scantlebury is one of the Earth's most prolific Christian authors. I commend him for his passion, dedication, patience, and prophetic articulation of the book of Revelation, which will surely command your brain to attention.

As I read **"Understanding the Revelation,"** I was challenged to grow as I learned more about God's Word with the turning of each page. As you read, I pray the same is true for you.

Apostle David M. Young Sr.
Lead Pastor,
Prevailing Word World Outreach Center,
New Castle, PA. USA
Fatherhood Specialist,
Children's Advocacy Center of Lawrence County

Introduction

As we embark on this study, there are certain things that we need to first establish. Here are five things that I believe the book of Revelation is about:

1. Revelation is the most Biblical book in the Bible.
2. Revelation has a system of symbolism.
3. Revelation is a prophecy about imminent events – events that were about to break loose on the world of the First Century.
4. Revelation is a worship service.
5. Revelation is a book about dominion.

Also, we have to study The Revelation as a part of the entirety of Scripture and not as a separate book on its own. It ties in beautifully with the rest of the Bible and Israel's journey. So, as we study the prophecy within this book, we will see how it ties in with Jesus' prophecy in Matthew 24 and many of the words spoken directly to the tribes of Israel. It was a powerful and very relevant book for the First Century Church and gives us today a clear picture of God's way of dealing with His people. When approached from this point of view, fresh realms of understanding will herald some fresh and powerful truths for us today.

Also, we need to bear in mind that the Bible is a record of Two Covenants; the Old Covenant which had a shelf life and was destined to come to an end. And then we have the New Covenant which is eternal and as such will never end. It has been eternally established by our King and Lord, Jesus the Christ. We need to add to this the understand that the entire cannon of Scripture was written before AD 70.

Another item of great importance which needs to be considered is the issue of God's Wrath:

GOD'S WRATH

God was married to Old Covenant Israel as He had planned for them to be the prototype nation through which all nations and people groups would be saved. However, they played the harlot and committed many acts of adultery which was sacrilege to Him. Time and time again He forgave and took them back only to see them repeat the same acts of disobedience and disloyalty. Father God eventually came in the Person of His Son Jesus Christ to seek their love, loyalty, and commitment to purity once and for all, but they once again turned on Him and sided with Caesar and the Roman authorities to have Jesus killed.

From that time God decided that He would come true on His promise not only to divorce them but to completely annihilate them. So, His wrath was poured out on them. As a matter of fact, much of the prophecy of the book of Revelation describes this wrath of God being poured out on Old Covenant Israel.

So, once we understand that the symbol of the Old Covenant system was destroyed circa AD 70 with the full establishment of His New Covenant Bride also known as the Church, we would realize that His wrath had ceased. Now, we who live in this New Covenant era are not the recipients of God's wrath.

I believe the next time we will witness God's wrath in full display would be at the end of human history when He judges the entire world and at that time, He will cast the devil and all those who chose to follow him in the lake of fire for all of eternity. That will be His last act of wrath and vengeance.

So, as we continue to live and serve Him, we are being used to assist in causing His Kingdom rule to spread throughout the nations of the earth. We have been forgiven and He has made provision for us to be forgiven and restored if we ever fall into sin. His wrath has already been poured out on Old Covenant Israel and we are living in the Day of God's Favour and His Grace. So, let us boldly proclaim His Will and Agenda across every sphere of human life. And finally, we must learn and understand what the Scriptures teach us about the coming of Jesus (and there were a few) as this will allow us to accurately view the teachings. I believe that there have been many comings of Jesus and that the Bible does not teach us about a specific 'Second Coming'. I believe that He came as He promised in AD 70 in judgment on the Old Covenant Jerusalem and that He will come again at the end of human history when the final judgment occurs. And no one knows when exactly it would occur. Many have guessed and sold everything and have waited in fields for His appearing, but all of this has not played out for these sincere but misled Believers. As we have seen from this folly of predicting the "Second Coming" of Jesus, in the same breath let me also say that we cannot believe or teach on any facts such as a "Second Coming" unless provable by Scripture.

I do believe that the earth will not end or be destroyed but that human history has a final chapter and an end, but no one knows when that shall be. And no one knows what shall be after that final chapter. I would venture to say that Heaven most likely will fully occupy earth and that we will reign in the universe with God from here.

I also believe this was revealed to Daniel in his interpreting King Nebuchadnezzar's dream (see Daniel 2). Because he saw the Kingdom coming into the earth as a small stone with power and authority to completely smash and destroy the king's image and then it grew and grew until it filled the entire earth. From this I believe that the Kingdom of God is ordained to rule the entire earth and to finally base His Headquarters here on this planet, just as He did in the Garden of Eden.

We need to firmly believe and understand that the entire New Testament was written before AD 70 and the destruction of the physical Jewish Temple. And here is the reason why: because Jesus had prophesied to His early disciples that the Temple and Jerusalem was going to be destroyed within a generation, they knew that life for them was going to be short. And as such they lived with an expectation of His coming within their lifetime to do what He said would occur. They did not think or plan long term. Think about that for a moment: If you knew that Jesus was coming within your generation what would you have done? Exactly, you would not make plans for any long term stay upon the earth. You would not be thinking about your grandchild's future and storing up for them. No, you would make sure that everything was right in your life and that of your immediate family's life.

While many liberal theologians would say differently, John A.T. Robinson has written a masterpiece that correctly demonstrates that the entire New Testament was written before the AD 70 destruction of Jerusalem.[1] This context is important because it gives a foundation for interpreting the New Testament. With that truth in mind, we can understand that the backdrop to everything recorded in the New Testament was the impending doom that was about to fall upon the city of Jerusalem. Consider these few examples:

Why would the early disciples sell their property? (See Acts 4:32–37.) They did this because they had insider information that the city was about to be destroyed.

- What was Stephen accused of that led to his stoning? (See Acts 6:13–14.) Stephen was declaring the impending destruction. (A false witness typically meant a bribed witness.)
- Why, instead of building large churches, did the early Church chose to meet in the temple courts and from house to house? (See Acts 2:46.) They did this because they knew their city was about to be destroyed. If you knew destruction was coming, would you start building a large church facility? Of course not! Instead, you would logically meet in homes and lecture halls (see Acts 2:46; 19:9).
- Why did James encourage his readers to take their plans lightly? (See James 4:13–17.) He did this because he knew that at any moment the destruction of Jerusalem could begin (see James 5:1–9).

Here is a quote from Jonathan Welton in his book "Raptureless" a book I am totally in agreement with and in the following lines, it is quoted here with permission:

[2]When the New Testament refers to Jesus' coming, it is a clear reference to the impending judgment upon Jerusalem in AD 70. Once we

---

[1] John A. T. Robinson, Redating the New Testament (SCM Press, 2012).
[2] Welton, Jonathan. Raptureless: An Optimistic Guide to the End of the World - Revised Edition Including The Art of Revelation. BookBaby. Kindle Edition.

understand that, we can shine light upon the passages that are used to teach the any-moment return of Christ:

Therefore be on the alert, for you do not know which day your Lord is coming (Matthew 24:42).

Be on the alert then, for you do not know the day nor the hour (Matthew 25:13).

Be on guard! Be alert! You do not know when that time will come (Mark 13:33).

But let us be alert and sober (1 Thessalonians 5:6b).

The First Century Christians had to be prepared for and watchful of the impending judgment. We are informed through the historical record that not one Christian died in the destruction of Jerusalem. To put that in context, 1.1 million Jews were killed in the slaughter, but every Christian of the First Century understood that the prophecy of Matthew 24 was about their generation, and they literally kept watch and ran for the mountains of Pella to escape the destruction.

In Matthew 24:15–18, Jesus gave very practical advice to His followers about how to stay alive during the AD 70 destruction. We can tell from this passage that Jesus was speaking of a local destruction (flee Judea) and a historical setting (not on a Sabbath). The natural tendency, upon seeing an approaching army, would have been to flee into Jerusalem for safety. Yet Jesus told them to fight their natural instincts and flee the city. Because of Jesus' command to flee, His followers were protected. It was important for the first-generation Church to be alert and watchful so that they wouldn't die in the AD 70 destruction. These verses applied to them, but they do not apply to us. We are not called to live on the edge of our seats believing Jesus could come at any moment. We are called to pray it would be *"on earth as it is in heaven"* (Matthew 6:10). We are to occupy until He comes, not be preoccupied with His coming!

This is why the Christians of today do not need to live with an "any moment Christ would return mentality" and could plan long term. We could invest in legacies that would last for generations without any fear.

We could build large meeting facilities and plan on store up an inheritance for our children and our children's children. I hope you are 'seeing' what I am saying.

We have to live like King David, who stored up vast resources of wealth for his son Solomon to build during his reign. You can refer to his story in the account of 1 Chronicles 22. David was thinking way in advance of his time for future generations and the fact that Temple of God needed to be built, although he knew that he wasn't going to be alive to witness it.

We learn from King Solomon, who wrote the Book of Proverbs, *"A righteous man leaves an inheritance for his children's children"* (Proverbs 13:22). It is very significant that Solomon was able to write this proverb because of witnessing his father, King David, living as a righteous man and thinking of his children's children. This proverb is not simply a wise saying; it was something Solomon observed and appreciated about his father, the righteous King David.

The larger context of the Bible teaches that the righteous think long term. Yet much of modern Christianity has been infected with short-term thinking. Consider the following quote from The Days of Vengeance:

First, have you ever wondered why Christians in the United States are clearly in the majority, and always have been, yet they have so little cultural influence? Here are three good reasons:

1. They have no plan.
2. They have little or no personal incentive.
3. They see no long-run hope of success.[3]

Although there are moments in time, such as AD 70, when God gave a warning and told the early Christians to keep watch, this is not to be the posture of all Christians for all time. We are not called to live on the edge of our seats and bite our nails hoping for (or fearing) the 'rapture'. Actually, for much of Church history, Christian leaders have taught and believed we are called to think and live long-term. Take, for example, the Book of Common Prayer. We can see from the fact that it contains tables for finding Holy Days all the way through AD 8400 that its compilers were not expecting Christ to return in the near future![4] This is just one example

---

[3] Gary North, preface to David Chilton, The Days of Vengeance (Dallas, GA: Dominion Press, 1987), xvi.
[4] "Tables for Finding Holy Days," The Book of Common Prayer (1662).

from a multitude throughout history that the idea of thinking long-term and building the Kingdom of God in the earth realm until the final return of Christ has been the predominant view of the Church in history. Also consider the words of the following leaders:

> All unprejudiced persons may see with their eyes, that He is already renewing the face of the earth: And we have strong reason to hope that the work He hath begun He will carry on unto the day of the Lord Jesus; that He will never intermit this blessed work of His Spirit until He has fulfilled all His promises, until He hath put a period to sin and misery, and infirmity, and death; and re-established universal holiness and happiness, and caused all the inhabitants of the earth to sing together "Hallelujah." —John Wesley[5]

> The visible kingdom of satan shall be overthrown, and the Kingdom of Christ set up on the ruins of it, everywhere throughout the whole habitable globe. —Jonathan Edwards[6]

> I, myself believe that King Jesus will reign, and the idols be utterly abolished; but I expect the same power which turned the world upside down once, will still continue to do it. The Holy Ghost would never suffer the imputation to rest upon His holy name that He was not able to convert the world. —Charles Spurgeon[7]

Once we settle into the fact that the Kingdom has been here since the Manger in Bethlehem and is growing and being established more and more through the Church here on earth, we can begin to understand our calling. The Church no longer needs to live on the edge of her seat, as if she will float away any second! She no longer has to wait with an identity crisis—"Why won't my groom come back for me?" Instead, she can get on with her calling to build the Kingdom of God upon the earth. For this reason, it is vitally and profoundly important that the Church abandon the any-moment-return doctrine and embrace the long-term thinking of the righteous person (see Proverbs 13:22).

---

[5] The Works of John Wesley (Nashville, TN: Abingdon Press, Volume 2, 1985), 499.
[6] The Works of Jonathan Edwards (London, England: Banner of Truth Trust, 1974), 488.
[7] Henry Davenport Northrop, Life and Work of Charles Haddon Spurgeon (Chicago: Monarch Book Company, 1890), 4:210.

As citizens of Heaven (see Philippians 3:20) and as ambassadors of Heaven (see 2 Corinthians 5:20), we are here with a mission. Jesus is not coming back until we finish the Apostolic Mission—the mission of the Apostolos to implement the culture of Heaven into the culture of the earth.

Someday the Church will complete this mission. Sons and daughters of King Jesus will know who they are and will live out their identity as righteous people. Suffering will be brought to a minimum in the earth realm. Sin will massively decrease. People will live longer, healthier, and more joy-filled lives. All the enemies of God will bow under Jesus' feet until finally death is put under His feet as the last foe (see 1 Corinthians 5:26). All other foes will be subdued as we put them under our feet (see Romans 16:20).

The day will come when the culturing of the Apostolos has completed the Apostolic Mission. Then, Jesus will be able to touch His feet upon earth in bodily form and finally say, as the Roman Emperors did in days past, "This place feels a lot like home!"[8]

With this understanding we can now move on to our first chapter – "Understanding the Revelation".

---

[8] Welton, Jonathan. Raptureless: An Optimistic Guide to the End of the World - Revised Edition Including The Art of Revelation. BookBaby. Kindle Edition.

CHAPTER ONE
DATING THE REVELATION

DATING THE REVELATION (PARAPHRASED FROM DR. JOHN NOE)
THE ACTUAL MOMENT IN TIME WHEN THE BOOK OF THE REVELATION WAS GIVEN to John the Apostle on the isle of Patmos is of critical importance in unlocking its mysteries. Unfortunately, scholars have reached different conclusions after assessing the dating evidence. The majority contends for a date around A.D. 95 or 96. This date is termed the "late date." But a sizeable and growing minority feels the Revelation was written prior to the destruction of both the Temple and the city of Jerusalem's in A.D. 70. This is termed the "early date."

I believe that adherence to the late date effectively rules out any contemporary and significant historical event as the soon-coming fulfillment or any relevance for its original and named recipients [those to whom this book was specifically written to, although it holds great significance to us here living in the 21st Century. Especially as many Believers today are still looking for a 'rapture' to occur and an anti-christ to manifest. Both leading to an incorrect interpretation of the Scriptures]. However, with the acceptance of the early date, this opens the possibility that it describes those events leading up to and including Jerusalem's fall and the destruction of the Temple in A.D. 70.

Notably, Philip Schaff, who wrote *History of the Christian Church* in eight volumes, and in the Preface to his Revised Edition, admits that "on two points I have changed my opinion – the second Roman captivity of

Paul . . . and the date of the Apocalypse (which I now assign, with the majority of modern critics, to the year 68 or 69 instead of 95, as before)"[9]

Most interestingly, the major piece of dating evidence cited by the popular late-date theorists is an ambiguous and questionable passage written by Irenaeus, one of the early Church fathers who wrote around A.D. 180-190. But translation difficulties, precludes this passage from being used as evidence. Moreover, Irenaeus said nothing about the date of the writing of Revelation. The bigger issue with Irenaeus, however, is his credibility. He claimed that Jesus' earthly ministry lasted approximately fifteen years and that Jesus lived to be almost fifty years old. Thus, the difficulties with Irenaeus' writings in this dating matter are many and varied.

On the other hand, and in our opinion, arguments for the early date are superior, both quantitatively and qualitatively, to those advanced for the late date. For example, of the two types of dating evidence, scholars generally acknowledge internal evidence (contained inside a document) as preferable and taking precedence over external evidence (what others, like Irenaeus, have said about a document).

John A.T. Robinson in his book *Redating the New Testament* points out that Revelation, along with all New Testament books, says nothing about the destruction of Jerusalem and the Temple in A.D. 70. He terms this omission as "one of the oddest facts," and questions why this event "is never once mentioned as a past fact" by any New Testament book, even though it is "predicted" and "would appear to be the single most datable and climactic event of the period" (John A.T. Robinson, *Redating the New Testament* (Philadelphia, PA.: Westminster Press, 1976) 13).

This omission propelled Robinson's re-dating study. His hypothesis and eventual conclusion was that "the whole of the New Testament was written before 70." He places the writing of Revelation in A.D. 68 (Ibid., 10, 352). Admittedly, Robinson's argument is an argument from silence. But those who claim that Revelation was written in AD 95-96 do have major difficulties explaining this omission.[10]

---

[9] (Philip Schaff, *History of the Christian Church*, Vol. 1, (Grand Rapids, MI.: Eerdmans, 1910 [third revision]) *vi*, also 420, 834n).

[10] https://www.prophecyrefi.org/our-teachings/book-of-revelation/when-was-it-most-likely-written/

Chapter One: Dating the Revelation

[11]WHEN WAS IT OR WILL IT BE FULFILLED?

The book of Revelation does not contain end-of-the-world predictions or events, as is commonly held. Rather, it fully predicted and described, symbolically and accurately, the events leading up to and including the fall of Jerusalem in a coming of the day of the Lord, in judgment, and in the change of covenants, in A.D. 70. All this and more occurred "soon" and "shortly"—i.e., within two to seven years, depending upon the exact date of this book's writing. Any interpretation of its fulfillment that lies beyond the time frame of its original hearers and readers is, at best, suspect.

Again, first and foremost, the book of Revelation described a local series of events very near to its writing and intended for an original and primary audience. These all occurred. Mistakenly, however, many feel that these events were only local and not worldwide. But just like the birth, life, death, resurrection, and ascension of Jesus, which were also local events, the Revelation's fulfillment has universal applications and implications. Locally is just how God is choosing to fulfill it and his plan of redemption.

These events ended, forever, biblical Judaism, its age, and the old covenant system (Hebrews 8:13; 9:10).

Reluctantly, the late, renowned, and futuristic theologian George Eldon Ladd conceded that "there must be an element of truth in this approach, for surely the Revelation was intended to speak to its own generation" (Ladd, *A Theology of the New Testament*, 672). Mistakenly, however, he and many others feel that if this prophecy is totally fulfilled, this makes it meaningless to modern-day Christians. But as we are about to see, Revelation's past fulfillment does not exhaust its meaning, relevance, and symbolism. In fact, just the opposite is true. Past fulfillment makes this prophecy *more meaningful*, not less. Why? It's because the Revelation is more than a tract for its own times. How can we know this? It's not some doctrine we have dreamed up, which leads us to our fifth foundational key for unlearning many popular misconceptions and unlocking the mysteries of this vital book.

AUDIENCE RELEVANCE

So, as we study the Word of God, we must use this master key – Audience Relevance. And we do this by asking a few questions such as:

---

[11] https://www.prophecyrefi.org/our-teachings/book-of-revelation/when-was-it-or-will-it-be-fulfilled/

1. To whom was this passage or letter written to?
2. Why was it written?
3. How did those to whom it was written understood it?
4. Then we can ask – how does this apply to me? How could I benefit from it?

And I am sure that there are other questions that can be asked. However, this is a good place to begin. You would gain much more from your time of study as you do!

As we continue, I would like for us to visit the first and last chapters of the book [its bookend if you will] of Revelation. However, before doing so let us take a look at the name of this letter. Remember the title for this letter "The Revelation" is translated from the Greek language, the language it was originally written in. The Strong's concordance reveals that the Greek word used is the word apokalypses, pronounced (ä-po-kä'-lü-pses) meaning: —appearing, coming, lighten, manifestation, be revealed, revelation.

It was written as a disclosure of truth and instruction concerning divine things which were once unknown — especially those relating to Christian salvation — given to the soul by God Himself, or by the ascended Christ, especially through the operation of the Holy Spirit (1 Corinthians 2:10 *"God has revealed to us through the Spirit. For the Spirit searches everything, even the depths of God."*).

In order to be distinguished from other methods of instruction as stated in Ephesians 3:3 *how the mystery was made known to me by revelation, as I have written briefly."* It was a spirit received from God disclosing what and how great are the benefits of salvation as per the following outlined in Ephesians 1:17.

That the God of our Lord Jesus Christ, the Father of glory, may give you a spirit of wisdom and of revelation in the knowledge of him,

Let us now look at the first and last chapters of the book of Revelation:

Revelation 1:1
The Revelation of Jesus Christ, which God gave Him to show His servants—things which must shortly take place. And He sent and signified it by His angel to His servant John,

Chapter One: Dating the Revelation

Revelation 22:20-21
He who testifies to these things says, "Surely I am coming quickly." Amen. Even so, come, Lord Jesus! The grace of our Lord Jesus Christ be with you all. Amen.

[12] Much of the conflict and confusion over the Revelation stems from just such a practice of taking part or all of this prophecy out of its divinely determined time context, stretching it like a rubber band by nineteen centuries and counting, plopping it down out into the future, and creating a pretext for its fulfillment. But disregarding or abusing context is not the prerogative of any sincere reader or honest interpreter.

The Book of Revelation places its own direct and contextualizing time statements upon the whole of its prophecy. Like bookends at its beginning and end (its first and last chapters/introduction and conclusion/prologue and epilogue), these time statements establish the historical framework for the soon and now past fulfillment of the whole prophecy.

These bookends to the book of Revelation gives us the urgency of the message contained in this book to its original readers. It also reveals to us who is the Source of the revelation contained in this book. In the opening verse we read that it is the Revelation of Jesus Christ, which God gave Him to show to His servants. And then the final verse of this book reveals that once again Jesus declares to the original readers over 2,000 years ago *"Surely I am coming quickly."*

The strategic placement of these bookends brackets the entire prophecy and was done, no doubt, to avoid confusion. So, from this we know that what is contained in the revelation of this book had very significant meaning to its first recipients – the First Century Believers.

But most commentators and prophecy teachers have missed, dismissed, or ignored these time and contextualizing statements, as well as their strategic placement:

- *"what must soon [shortly] take place"* (Revelation 1:1; 22:6 [KJV]).
- *"Blessed is the one who reads the words of this prophecy ... who hear it and take to heart [obey] what is written in it"* (Revelation 1:3; 22:7 [KJV]).
- *"the time is near [at hand]"* (Revelation 1:3; 22:10 [KJV]).

---

[12] Dating the book of Revelation: John Noe, The Greater Jesus: His glorious unveiling (pp. 97-98, 104). East2West Press. Kindle Edition. (Paraphrased)

- *"Do not seal up the words of the prophecy of this book"* (Revelation 22:10). Note: Daniel was told to *"close up and seal the words"* of his book *"until the time of the end"* (Daniel 12:4). In the Revelation, that time was now *"near"* or *"at hand."*
- *"Behold, I am coming soon [quickly]!"* (Revelation 22:7, 12 [KJV]).
- *"Yes, I am coming soon [quickly]."* (Revelation 22:20 [KJV]).

Once again, these full-content-bracketing time statements establish the immediate historical context for the fulfillment of the whole of the prophecy. When ignored, as so many have done, it's easy to lose sight of the proverbial "forest for the trees." (*End of paraphrase*).

What is needed is a careful, honest, and consistent approach—one that preserves the integrity and harmony of the whole of the prophecy and its associated events. Arbitrary divisions and specialized or alternative meanings of common and ordinarily understood words have no part in this process. The simplest solution is to recognize that the whole of the prophecy was written, first and foremost, to 1st Century Christians.

Now there are basically four views people use for revelation when reading the book of Revelation that I would like for us to explore before going forward: Idealism, Futurism, Historicism, and Preterism. Each of these views of interpretation answer the basic four questions—when, how, why, and where—very differently.

Paraphrased from Jonathan Welton's book "The Art of Revelation"

To understand this, let's imagine four experts standing in front of the Book of Revelation, and each expert has been trained by one of these four schools of thought. A passerby joins the group of experts and begins to ask the four important questions in hopes of understanding this book.

He begins with the first question: "When was this book written?" The Preterist responds first. "It was likely painted during the reign of Nero, based on the prophecy about seven kings listed in Revelation 17. It was written regarding the AD 70 destruction of Jerusalem, and as a prophecy of that event, it was written in advance of that event."

Then the Idealist, Futurist, and Historicist chime in together. "It doesn't really matter when it was written," they say, "because the content is prophetic. It is probably about distant events and mysterious symbols.

The novice then introduces his second question, "How was this book written?" he asks. "What reasoning and understanding did the writer use?" Once again, the Preterist quickly speaks, saying, "Revelation was written in the same manner as the books of Ezekiel, Jeremiah, and Isaiah, which all describe the first destruction of Jerusalem in 586 BC. John chose this style because of the AD 70 destruction of the temple."

The other three nodded in mild agreement, and then voice their differences. "We do agree that Revelation is full of Old Testament symbolism and imagery, yet we definitely do not agree that John wrote it this way because of the AD 70 destruction of the temple."

The Idealist adds, "John chose these symbols to point to the ongoing spiritual cosmic struggle between the kingdom of darkness and the kingdom of light, in which light ultimately wins." "I'd say, instead, that he cloaked all of Church history in mysterious symbolism centuries before it would unfold as it has and continues to unfold," the Historicist says.

Finally, the Futurist adds his point of view. "I agree that there are symbols and Old Testament references, but I believe that it will all make sense someday in the future when these events begin."

"All this is very interesting," the novice says. "But why did the writer pen this book?" This time, the Historicist chimes in first. "John was compelled to write all of human history into one book. He penned it in advance of all the major coming events, centuries ahead of time. This has always been the nature of prophecy."

The Futurist shook his head, saying, "I believe John was transported in a vision to the distant future, and when he returned from his vision, he recorded all that he witnessed about the time of the end of human history."

After quietly thinking for a few moments, the Idealist says, "I disagree with you both. John was a very mystical man. We see this from his strange Gospel account, which is so very different from the other three. I believe John wanted to show the cosmic struggle and the victory of Jesus in grand splendor."

At last, the Preterist speaks. "I keep telling you guys, the Early Church was surviving under brutal persecution, and in that context, John said his writing was understandable (Revelation 13:18) and a blessing (Revelation 1:3; 22:7) to those who saw it. If his writing was about the distant future or served as an overlay of Church history, how would this encourage them? I believe the Christians in the First Century knew exactly what John's writing meant."

"Ok. I can see the four of you don't agree on much," says the novice, chuckling. "Perhaps you can give me an answer to my final question: Where was the book written? What location does it reference?"

"The Revelation," says the Idealist, "represents the heavenly realm and is written with all the spiritual pictures and components expected of a story about the battle between light and darkness."

"I disagree," says the Futurist. "The location referred to in the Revelation is the planet earth in the future."

The Historicist then adds his perspective. "The location isn't so important, considering that this has been unfolding and will continue to unfold over time. Although the city with seven hills is probably Rome, (Revelation 17:9) and Babylon the Harlot is probably the Roman Catholic Church."

The Preterist answers last, saying, "The numbers, dimensions, measurements, and specifics that are recorded in the Revelation all made perfect sense to First Century Christians. There was very little mystery to the imagery that John used to convey his message to his intended audience. Only as the dust of Church history has settled has this writing become more mysterious."

The other three stare in disbelief at the Preterist, who always seemed to be proposing the most unusual ideas. Our bystander novice smiles and thanks his expert friends.

"Clearly," he says, "there are four different ways to look at this writing. Now I will have to decide which one I like the best."

This imaginary dialogue gives us a basic understanding of each of these viewpoints. In the next chapter, we will examine the answers to the bystander's four important questions more closely. These questions are the key to helping us see the big picture of Revelation. [End of paraphrase]

The Latest Picture of Jesus

The first chapter of the Book of Revelation (the Apocalypse) unveils and reveals the latest and only full-blown, physically descriptive picture of Jesus in the Bible. By inspiration, John records what he heard and saw when Jesus literally and physically came, appeared, touched, spoke to, and commissioned him on the island of Patmos over nineteen hundred years ago:

> *I, John, your brother and companion in the suffering and kingdom and patient endurance that are ours in Jesus, was on the island of*

Patmos because of the word of God and the testimony of Jesus. On the Lord's Day I was in the Spirit, and I heard behind me a loud voice like a trumpet, which said: "Write on a scroll what you see and send it to the seven churches: to Ephesus, Smyrna, Pergamum, Thyatira, Sardis, Philadelphia, and Laodicea. I turned around to see the voice that was speaking to me. And when I turned I saw seven golden lampstands, and among the lampstands was someone "like a son of man," dressed in a robe reaching down to his feet and with a golden sash around his chest. His head and hair were white like wool, as white as snow, and his eyes were like blazing fire. His feet were like bronze glowing in a furnace, and his voice was like the sound of rushing waters. In his right hand he held seven stars, and out of his mouth came a sharp double-edged sword. His face was like the sun shining in all its brilliance. (Revelation 1:9-16)

Make no mistake; this is Jesus as He is now! We are not told the meaning of the sword coming out of his mouth or why his hair is white and his eyes like blazing fire. Nor are we told why a crown of thorns no longer encircles his head. But one thing is sure. He is no longer the Jesus of popular thought and tradition. He is that of course, but He is now much more. Grasping the full reality of this divinely revealed and new image of Jesus and knowing and serving Him as He is today, and as He requires, are essential prerequisites if we hope to hear the words someday, *"Well done, good and faithful servant"* (Matthew 25:21, 23; Revelation 1:3; 22:7). Anything less is less.

But tell me, where is this image of Jesus being presented, nowadays? Where is this picture of today's Christ hanging on a wall? Where is this present-day and pertinent perspective being taught, studied, and worshiped? Since the time John personally saw and experienced Jesus like this, Jesus has not changed. Therefore, we can definitely affirm that *"Jesus Christ is the same yesterday and today and forever"* (Hebrews 13:8). That is, He is the same in his Personhood and Divinity—the Second Person of the Trinity.

Critical Objection: Some theologians contend that the word "yesterday" means Jesus has never changed from His pre-existence before creation and ever since.[13] That assertion, however, is only partially true as

---

[13] The Greek word translated "yesterday" is chthes. For its two other uses, see John 4:52 and Acts 7:28. Hebrews 13:8 is literally correct as it reads.

William Hendriksen properly explains: "He is the same Saviour, yet different from the days of his humiliation."[14] The Greek word translated "yesterday" is chthes. For its two other uses, see John 4:52 and Acts 7:28. Hebrews 13:8 is literally correct as it reads. William Hendriksen, More than Conquerors (Grand Rapids, MI.: Baker Book House, 1940, 1962, 1982).

I would like you to see and understand what I am about to say before going forward: Jesus always existed within His Eternal Father, who has no beginning or end, He is Eternal, always was and always will be. The natural earthly Jesus as the Son of God had a beginning and an end. As you would recall He was born of the virgin Mary who was impregnated by God's Holy Spirit. So, there is a natural, earthly dimension to Jesus. There is no denying this, but we have to understand that He is not like that anymore and that is not the Jesus we need to worship. This Jesus was necessary to enter the earth realm and become the Saviour of humankind, because we all know or should know that God will not use any other form to work through upon the earth. When He created Adam, God set the stage for the one through whom He would work in the earth realm.

After Adam and Eve gave up their birthright to the devil God worked through the ages to get a perfect man that He could work through, but He could not find any because all were born in sin and shaped in iniquity. It was not until He decided to come in the Person of His Son Jesus the Christ to live a perfect human life and then to willingly go to the Cross and lay down His life for the sins of the human race did God finally find the Perfect man He desired. However, this same Jesus after He rose from the grave came into His pre-human manifested form into His true image that we must now worship as the Christ, Jesus the Son of the Living God. Once again here is His eternal description: Revelation 1:10-16

> I was in the Spirit on the Lord's day, and I heard behind me a loud voice like a trumpet saying, "Write what you see in a book and send it to the seven churches, to Ephesus and to Smyrna and to Per'gamum and to Thyati'ra and to Sardis and to Philadelphia and to La-odice'a." Then I turned to see the voice that was speaking to me, and on turning I saw seven golden lampstands, *and in the midst of the lampstands one like a son of man, clothed with a long robe and with a golden girdle round his breast; his head and his*

---
[14] William Hendriksen, More that Conquerors (Grand Rapids, MI.: Baker Book House, 1940, 1962, 1982), 56.

hair were white as white wool, white as snow; his eyes were like a flame of fire, his feet were like burnished bronze, refined as in a furnace, and his voice was like the sound of many waters; in his right hand he held seven stars, from his mouth issued a sharp two-edged sword, and his face was like the sun shining in full strength. (Emphasis Author's)

I submit to you that this is the Jesus as He was yesterday, today, and forever. Yes, the historical Jesus is very important, but we don't need to worship Him like that anymore. He finished His human assignment and has stepped back into His eternal place with the Father. Are you seeing this?

In the next chapter we will explore the breakdown of the Revelation.

CHAPTER TWO
BREAKDOWN OF THE REVELATION

THE BOOK OF REVELATION IS COMPRISED OF NINE MAIN ELEMENTS—AN introduction, seven visions, and an epilogue. Here's the breakdown:

- The Introduction (Revelation 1:1–7)
- First Vision—The Seven Churches (Revelation 1:8–3:22)
- Second Vision—The Seven Seals (Revelation 4:1–8:5)
- Third Vision—The Seven Trumpets (Revelation 8:6–11:19)
- Fourth Vision—Followers of the Lamb or the beast (Revelation 12–14)
- Fifth Vision—The Seven Bowls of Wrath (Revelation 15-16)
- Sixth Vision—The Babylonian Harlot (Revelation 17–19:21)
- Seventh Vision—The New Heavens and New Earth (Revelation 20:1–22:11)
- The Epilogue (Revelation 22:12–21) These nine components are the main focus of the remainder of this book.

Revelation begins with John's announcement of its name, The Revelation of Jesus Christ, and His promise that the events prophesied within it were designated to happen very soon. Then, he shares his first dramatic vision, in which the risen Christ appears to him. This vision is separate from the out-of-body experiences that John records in Revelation 4–22.

Here in chapter 1, John is on the island of Patmos and he records that Jesus walked up behind him. John records that encounter as follows:

Revelation: 1:12-18
Then I turned to see the voice that was speaking to me, and on turning I saw seven golden lampstands, and in the midst of the lampstands one like a son of man, clothed with a long robe and with a golden girdle round his breast; his head and his hair were white as white wool, white as snow; his eyes were like a flame of fire, his feet were like burnished bronze, refined as in a furnace, and his voice was like the sound of many waters; in his right hand he held seven stars, from his mouth issued a sharp two-edged sword, and his face was like the sun shining in full strength. When I saw him, I fell at his feet as though dead. But he laid his right hand upon me, saying, "Fear not, I am the first and the last, and the living one; I died, and behold I am alive for evermore, and I have the keys of Death and Hades.

As we read through this account, it is very important for us to fully understanding the seven letters that follow in Revelation chapters 2–3. Jesus appears to John as He is today, and He instructed John to write to the seven churches.

Jesus is completely different from the human Jesus that walked the face of the earth and died on the Cross for the sins of mankind. He is now revealed as He is today. This is the Jesus that we need to know and the Jesus that we need to worship. Again, here is His current description:

- He is clothed with a long robe and with a golden girdle round His breast
- His head and His hair were white as white wool, white as snow.
- His eyes were like flaming fire
- His feet were like burnished bronze, refined as in a furnace, and
- His voice was like the sound of many waters
- In His right hand He held seven stars, from His mouth issued a sharp two-edged sword, and
- His face was like the sun shining in full strength

As we continue reading this letter that was spoken to John, we see that there were specific instructions given to seven churches. Please remember that the establishment and building of this new Temple of God called the Church was new. John received this vision within the first generation after Jesus' death, burial, and ascension. So, these were real churches and not as some believe to be seven church ages. We need to be able to establish this fact before going forward.

Let us now take a brief look at the seven churches to which the letter was sent. Jesus not only addresses the specific situation of each church, but He also reveals the visionary revelation of Himself that He has just shown to John. These self-descriptions which appear at the beginning of each letter are each a small selection from the larger description given in Revelation 1:12–18. It is the way Jesus chose to reveal Himself to each church and more details as to His instructions to each of them follow in Revelation chapters 2–3.

1. Ephesus—He holds the seven stars and walks among the seven lampstands Revelation 2:1 *"To the angel of the church in Ephesus write: 'The words of him who holds the seven stars in his right hand, who walks among the seven golden lampstands."*
2. Smyrna—He is the First and Last, the Living One Revelation 2:8 *"And to the angel of the church in Smyrna write: 'The words of the first and the last, who died and came to life."*
3. Pergamum—He has the sharp, double-edged sword in His mouth Revelation 2:12, 16 *"And to the angel of the church in Per'gamum write: 'The words of him who has the sharp two-edged sword. Repent then. If not, I will come to you soon and war against them with the sword of my mouth."*
4. Thyatira—He is the Son of God, whose eyes are like fire and His feet like bronze Revelation 2:18 *"And to the angel of the church in Thyati'ra write: 'The words of the Son of God, who has eyes like a flame of fire, and whose feet are like burnished bronze."*
5. Sardis—He holds the seven spirits of God and the seven stars Revelation 3:1 *"And to the angel of the church in Sardis write: 'The words of him who has the seven spirits of God and the seven stars."*
6. Philadelphia—He is holy and true, and He holds the key of David Revelation 3:7 *"And to the angel of the church in Philadelphia write:*

'The words of the holy one, the true one, who has the key of David, who opens and no one shall shut, who shuts and no one opens."
7. Laodicea—He is the faithful and true witness, the ruler of God's creation (see Revelation 3:14 "And to the angel of the church in Laodice'a write: 'The words of the Amen, the faithful and true witness, the beginning of God's creation."

One of the things that we need to see and realize here is this. Jesus releases to John instructions that he is to give to these seven churches. However, we need to recognize that He is giving a full view of who He is currently to these seven churches who represented the totality of His Church at that point. He did not give it to one church, but to all seven, so we would have to read and understand Him from the writings to these seven churches. I see this as a powerful and beautiful revelation of the Christ. As a matter it reveals to us what Jesus had spoken to His other Apostles. For example, let's consider what He spoke to Apostle Paul as recorded in the following passages:

1 Corinthians 13:9 and Ephesians 4:16
For our knowledge is imperfect and our prophecy is imperfect;

from whom the whole body, joined and knit together by every joint with which it is supplied, when each part is working properly, makes bodily growth and upbuilds itself in love.

This reveals the beauty of the Body of Christ. We know in part as was revealed to Apostle Paul in 1 Corinthians 13:9 and this is further developed in Ephesians 4:16. This also reveals to us as the Body of Christ we must work together in manifesting the fullness of Jesus to the world.

[15]Paraphrased from The Art of Revelation by Jonathan Welton

Further, Jesus purposefully presents Himself to each of the churches in a way that was historically and culturally relevant to them. These statements were not just general facts about the nature of Christ; they were specific pieces of revelation intended to deeply connect with the hearts and situations of these churches. For example, Pergamum was the seat of the Roman capital in Asia Minor and Jesus reveals Himself as the One with a sword, the One wielding true authority on the earth.

---

[15] [Paraphrased from] Welton, Jonathan. The Art of Revelation. BookBaby. Kindle Edition.

To Thyatira which was a city where the metal trade was the hub of business, Jesus reveals Himself as the one whose eyes were like fire and whose feet were burnished bronze. Jesus knew exactly which revelation would be the most personal and meaningful to His readers. In the seven letters, Jesus delivers His prophecies in a very personal manner. He gives each church a piece of revelation regarding who He is and the descriptive terms and examples of his personhood and character were specifically applicable to them in their context and situation. This is a picture of how the gift of prophecy is used within the Body of Christ.

Further, by starting this book with this sort of personal prophecy, Jesus sets the tone for the rest of the prophecy as something that is written in the language and symbolism uniquely applicable and meaningful to the people it was being written for in the first century. After Jesus' great revelation of Himself to John, He makes an important statement that helps us understand the structure of the revelation of Christ more completely: "Write, therefore, what you have seen, what is now and what will take place later" (Revelation 1:19). This verse divides the content of Revelation into three parts: past, present, and future. The vision of Jesus in Revelation 1:1–18 that John had just seen was "what you have seen." That was the past. The letters to the seven churches in Revelation 2–3 was "what is now." This was the reality that existed in John's present. The material that John would see in the heavenlies, in Revelation 4–22, was "what will take place later." This transition from present to future is made clear by the invitation in Revelation 4:1,

"Come up here, and I will show you what must take place after this."

John only begins to see the future after he is pulled up into the heavenly realm. As mentioned previously, viewing these timeframes through a historical and contextual grid, we can see that the "what was" and the "what is" of Revelation 1–3 lead up to the "what will be" of the remainder of the book. These are the events of AD 70—the destruction of Jerusalem and the old covenant system. This was obvious to John's First Century readers; however, it has escaped many modern-day readers. The reason is simple. Revelation is deeply symbolic, and it uses symbols that would have been meaningful in the First Century Jewish context. But these once-clear symbols are mysterious to us because we live in a different era and culture.

The first step to decoding the symbolism of Revelation is acknowledging that it is symbolic. Some people argue that they take Revelation literally, but the reality is, it is impossible to take the book completely literally, because the entire planet would be destroyed by chapter 6, when the sun turns black and all the stars in the sky fall upon the earth. If such an event literally occurred, there would be no need for the remaining chapters of Revelation. Instead, we must acknowledge that the book is full of symbolism. We see this from the start, even in Jesus' description of Himself in chapter 1. He says:

The mystery of the seven stars that you saw in my right hand and of the seven golden lampstands is this: The seven stars are the angels of the seven churches, and the seven lampstands are the seven churches (Revelation 1:20).

Here Jesus plainly tells John that the stars and lampstands are symbolic. They are a mystery that must be interpreted, and He gives the interpretation. The seven lampstands symbolize the seven churches, and the seven stars in His right hand symbolize the angels of those churches. This might seem like a strange arrangement—having an Apostle write and deliver letters to spirit beings known as angels—until we realize that stars are used symbolically throughout the Bible to speak of local government, and the Greek word angelos, which is translated here as "angels," simply means "messenger or envoy."[16] Knowing this, we can gather that the seven stars/angels refer to the local leadership of the seven churches,[17] which we look at in depth in the next chapter.

---

[16] For example, Joseph's dream in Genesis 37:5–11 was instantly recognized as foretelling his ascendancy to a ruling position, not the literal sun, moon, and stars bowing down to him.

[17] [End of paraphrase] from Welton, Jonathan. The Art of Revelation. BookBaby. Kindle Edition.

CHAPTER THREE
A Deeper Look into the Messages to the Seven Churches - I

OK, SO LET US NOW TAKE A DEEPER DIVE INTO THE MESSAGES THAT JESUS GAVE TO John to relay to these seven churches!

> Revelation 2:2-7 the church in Ephesus:
> *"'I know your works, your toil and your patient endurance, and how you cannot bear evil men but have tested those who call themselves apostles but are not, and found them to be false; I know you are enduring patiently and bearing up for my name's sake, and you have not grown weary. But I have this against you, that you have abandoned the love you had at first. Remember then from what you have fallen, repent and do the works you did at first. If not, I will come to you and remove your lampstand from its place, unless you repent. Yet this you have, you hate the works of the Nicola'itans, which I also hate. He who has an ear, let him hear what the Spirit says to the churches. To him who conquers I will grant to eat of the tree of life, which is in the paradise of God.'"*

It is obvious that the Lord was pleased with the Church at Ephesus. There are several noteworthy characteristics that were instrumental in shaping the church at Ephesus:

- They were full of good deeds.
- They were hard workers and had the ability to preserve.
- They had zero tolerance for wicked men.
- They obviously hated false apostles as they tested those who claim to be Apostles.
- They endured great hardship for their stand in Christ and did not grow weary from the constant persecution.
- They also hated the practices of the Nicolaitans, which the Lord, Himself hated!

The practices [doctrine] of the Nicolaitans:

According to [18]Jay Atkinson, the doctrine of the Nicolaitans was mentioned in the Apocalypse of John to the Churches of Ephesus and Pergamos of the seven churches of Asia in Revelation Chapter 2. It is a symbolic name of a party that represents the hierarchy of a ruling class over the rest of the people, developing a *pecking order* of fleshly leadership. Jesus hates this and warns the people to repent or else *"I will come upon you quickly and will fight against them with the sword of my mouth."*

The root of the word Nicolaitans comes from Greek *nikao,* to conquer or overcome, and *laos,* which means people and which the word laity comes from. The two words together especially means the destruction of the people and refers to the earliest form of what we call a priestly order or clergy which later on in Church history divided people and allowed for leadership other than those led by the Spirit of the risen Lord.

Nicolaism was an early Christian sect mentioned twice in the Book of Revelation of the New Testament. The adherents were called Nicolaitans, Nicolaitanes, or Nicolaites. They were considered heretical by the mainstream Church. (Wikipedia) The definition of this practice would be applied to the Nicolaitans who were "those who prevail over the people." This clerical system later developed into the papal hierarchy of priests and clergy lording their power over the flock. The Council of Trent stated, "If anyone shall say that there is not in the Catholic Church a hierarchy established by the divine ordination, consisting of bishops, presbyters and ministers, let him be anathema."

The various ministries of the church are not in question here, but rather the separation of them into a powerful hierarchy controlling the

---

[18] Jay Atkinson of The Latter Rain: http://latter-rain.com/perspectives/testimony.htm

followers. This hierarchy gave them absolute power over their sheep. The men holding these positions were viewed as infallible by the Believers. This very idea was taken over by the Protestants with their own corruption of leadership roles and coverings. The church of Ephesus was commended for hating the deeds of the Nicolaitans. The wrong separation of the clergy from the laity is a great evil in God's sight and He hates the lust for religious power over others. There is an ungodly spiritual authority in the Church today, which is nothing more than the prideful spirit of control, manipulation, domination and intimidation and a rebellion of the rightful authority of God.[19]

Faithful Believers, who have put on Christ Jesus, are all God's laity. Peter in his Epistle 1 Peter 5:1-4 exhorted us to *"feed the flock of God which is among you, taking the oversight thereof, not for filthy lucre but of a ready mind. Neither as being lords over God's heritage but being examples to the flock. And when the chief shepherd shall appear, you shall receive a crown of glory that fades not away."*

Shepherds serve the sheep but the wolves that clothe themselves with so-called leadership and spiritual authority serve themselves all the while thinking that they are serving God which in essence makes them false christs. Early Church leaders were established as overseers, not as a ruling hierarchy. The Lord said it succinctly to His disciples in: Matthew 10:42-45

> *You know that they which are accounted to rule over the Gentiles exercise lordship over them and their great ones exercise authority upon them. But so shall it not be among you but whosoever will be great among you shall be your minister. And whosoever of you will be the chiefest shall be servant of all. For even the Son of man came not to be ministered unto but to minister and to give His life a ransom for many.*

I believe that this doctrine and the doctrine of Balaam are the teachings that allow false apostles and false prophets as well as false teachers and false ministers to infiltrate the flock of God.

Remember the Church that Jesus Christ is building is being built on Him and the doctrine that He releases by His Holy Spirit, to Apostles

---

[19] Jay Atkinson http://latter-rain.com/eschae/nicola.htm

and Prophets who in turn release it to the Teachers and Ministers in the Church. This was firmly established when the Church began in the Book of Acts: Acts 2:36-44

> *Therefore let all Israel be assured of this: God has made this Jesus, whom you crucified, both Lord and Christ." When* the people heard this, they were cut to the heart and said to Peter and the other apostles, "Brothers, what shall we do?" *Peter replied, "Repent and be baptized, every one of you, in the name of Jesus Christ for the forgiveness of your sins. And you will receive the gift of the Holy Spirit. The promise is for you and your children and for all who are far off-for all whom the Lord our God will call." With many other words he warned them; and he pleaded with them, "Save yourselves from this corrupt generation."* Those who accepted his message were baptized, *and about three thousand were added to their number that day.* They devoted themselves to the apostles' teaching and to the fellowship, to the breaking of bread and to prayer. *Everyone was filled with awe, and* many wonders and miraculous signs were done by the apostles. [Emphasis Author's]

When the Holy Spirit arrived on the Day of Pentecost and launched the Church, Apostle Peter was the first one used to preach Jesus Christ in order to ensure the authenticity of the revelation released to these early Believers. Of note is the fact the moment the people received the Word that Peter spoke, they were convicted and immediately entered into to the true Spirit of the Church and that of the early Apostles, when they addressed the Apostles as "Brothers" [verse 37]! This to me is very interesting as this was the very inception of the Church and the Twelve Apostles were referred to as Brothers by those now being saved. They immediately understood the fact that Apostle is more of a function than that of a title! They knew that there was an Apostolic Grace on Peter and the other Apostles, so they immediately submitted to them and sought advice and direction.

The outcome of this momentous occasion was that they were water baptized and they continued steadfastly in the Apostles' doctrine and fellowship!

The Apostles' doctrine was and still is the key to the proper construction and function of the Church of Jesus Christ. As such it was vital that this "Apostles' doctrine" i.e. the preaching and teaching of Jesus Christ be successfully and securely passed on from generation to generation.

The Apostle Paul had to go through a major time of purging before he could be mightily used of the Lord in assisting to build His Church. In his life pre-Christ, he was Saul, a zealous Jew and according to the Jewish law, he was blameless [Philippians 3:4-9]!

The Lord had to strike him down to "detoxify" him from his religious ways. While on the road to Damascus, Paul's mission to persecute the early Church was cut short as the Lord struck him blind. He had to be emptied of his present beliefs and to be now filled with the true Doctrine of Jesus Christ in order to be used mightily to build the Church of Jesus Christ. The Lord went through great lengths in ensuring that the authentic Gospel got to His Church, and He continues to do this.

The church at Ephesus was undoubtedly blessed due to the letters that Apostle Paul wrote to them as he painted such revelatory pictures of the Church to them. It would serve well for us to explore these descriptions as they would further assist in our understanding of the Church that Jesus Christ said He would build.

Ephesus was a luxurious and splendid eastern city but witchcraft with its black arts and idolatrous superstitions of the Orient were at the centre core. Ephesus could well be called "superstition city" as its people lived in a superstitious atmosphere. The Ephesians worshipped the Asiatic goddess Diana, and its supreme glory was the temple of Artemis or Diana, one of the Seven Wonders of the World, which made the city famous. Not only at Ephesus, but throughout all of Asia and the then known world, the multi-breasted statue of Diana was worshipped as the goddess of virginity and motherhood from the outset and this veneration of her as the great has transcended from this pagan god over into the veneration of Mary as a religious force among the members of the Roman Catholic Church.

Ephesus was the capital of pro-consular Asia, about 40 miles SE of Smyrna and was a wealthy metropolis during Apostle Paul's day. The word Ephesus means "desirable" and this was reflected in the fact that it was called "The Treasure House of Asia." Ephesus was a proud, rich, and busy port, known as the market of Asia Minor and in those days, trade followed the river valleys and Ephesus stood at the mouth of the Cayster commanding the richest hinterland in Asia Minor.

Under the shadow of the temple of Artemis [Diana], ghostly priests and miracle workers abounded. Between the occult worship of Artemis and the widespread practice of magic, the city was preoccupied with the black arts. The worship of Artemis included shameless and vile practices such as prostitution and mutilation in the rituals. This made the residents easy prey to false magicians and vulnerable to demonic penetration. There were also the famous charms and spells called "Ephesians' Letters" that guaranteed to bring protection on journeys, children to the childless, and success in love or business. With this fame, people from all over the world came to Ephesus to buy these magic parchments which they wore as amulets and charms. This was the backdrop of demonic activity and darkness that the Lord sent Apostle Paul in to establish the Ephesian church.

The letter of Paul to the Ephesians was written during his imprisonment at Rome and was carried by Tychicus on his journey to Asia. This was a church that had been born in revival. In Acts Chapters 18-20, we read of how Paul came to Ephesus and preached for three months in the synagogue. Although he was greatly opposed, God did a great work in the city. We read in Acts 19:20, *"So mightily grew the Word of God and prevailed."*

The church at Ephesus is the first of the seven candlesticks of the apocalypse. The church at Ephesus was more than a building where people gathered. It was a body of Believers that worshipped on the first day of the week and worked the rest of the week. The word *"labour"* describes the kind of working congregation they were. The word describes "toiling to the point of exhaustion." It speaks of a "strenuous and exhausting labour." They were such hard workers; they were completely exhausting themselves in the work of Lord. The Believers in Ephesus worked themselves to the state of exhaustion for the sake of Jesus. But their labour cost them something dear...

Also, remember at that time there were no church buildings or denominations so the Believers met in halls or homes or wherever they could. There was not one great central temple where they all met. Several small congregations under separate Eldership made up the Ephesians' church; but the letter is addressed to "The church at Ephesus" – one church with many congregations.

This was the backdrop from which the Apostle Paul so masterfully and explicitly expounded and explained the Church that Jesus Christ was building and the Church He wanted to see manifest in the church at Ephesus.

As one journeys through the verses of the letter to the Ephesians, we find several [20]descriptions of the Church which, reveals the multi-faceted nature of the Church that Jesus Christ is building. The first of these descriptions is in the fact that the Church is God's Assembly or Ecclesia!

And God placed all things under his feet and appointed him to be head over everything for the church... [Ephesians 1:22]

This first letter to the Ephesians is significant and meaningful for us today, because it shows the progression that happened from before the destruction of the Jewish temple in AD 70 to after AD 70. Before, the Believers were promised certain things; after AD 70, the Believers received the experience of these promises as the Bride of Christ. After the complete and final victory of AD 70, all Believers could at that time and as well as now are able to eat from the tree of life. We are not waiting for this promise or any of the other promises of these letters to be fulfilled. This pattern is repeated in the remaining six letters. As mentioned previously, though the promises are addressed to specific churches, they are meant for all the faithful Believers of the first century. Now, in the years since AD 70, their fulfillment applies to all Believers.

Revelation 2:9-11 the church at Smyrna:
I know your tribulation and your poverty (but you are rich) and the slander of those who say that they are Jews and are not, but are a synagogue of satan. Do not fear what you are about to suffer. Behold, the devil is about to throw some of you into prison, that you may be tested, and for ten days you will have tribulation. Be faithful unto death, and I will give you the crown of life. He who has an ear, let him hear what the Spirit says to the churches. He who conquers shall not be hurt by the second death.

Smyrna was a large, important city on the western coast of Asia Minor, famed for its schools of medicine and science. The words of Jesus

---

[20] The seven pictures or descriptions of the Church is borrowed from the author's gleaning from the book "Rediscovering God's Church" masterfully written by the late Derek Prince and published by Whitaker House; and used by permission.

to the church in Smyrna in Revelation 2:8-11 offer insight into the life of a First Century congregation, and there are many applications for today's Believers.

The message was from the Lord Jesus Christ: "These are the words of him who is the First and the Last, who died and came to life again" (Revelation 2:8). The identity of the first and the last and the resurrected one could only be Jesus Christ (see Revelation 22:13).

Jesus starts by acknowledging their trials: *"I know your afflictions and your poverty—yet you are rich! I know the slander of those who say they are Jews and are not but are a synagogue of satan"* (Revelation 2:9). In their physical poverty, however, the church of Smyrna was "rich" in that they had spiritual wealth that no one could take away (Matthew 6:20).

As for the identity of the *"synagogue of satan,"* there are a couple of views. One view maintains that this was a group of Gentiles who called themselves "Jews" (i.e., the chosen people of God). Instead of following Judaism, however, these self-proclaimed "people of God" worshiped the Roman emperor and spoke out against the Christians in Smyrna.

Another view is that the "synagogue of satan" was a group of physical Jews who followed tradition and the Mosaic Law yet in reality did not know God. They were "not" Jews in the sense that they did not have the faith of their father Abraham (Luke 3:8; John 8:40), and they were "of satan" in that they had rejected Jesus Christ (John 8:44). Jesus dealt with many such religious leaders, as did the apostle Paul (Matthew 23; Acts 18:6). In fact, Paul differentiates "true" (spiritual) Jews from those who can only claim a physical connection to Abraham: "A man is not a Jew if he is only one outwardly, nor is circumcision merely outward and physical. No, a man is a Jew if he is one inwardly; and circumcision is circumcision of the heart, by the Spirit, not by the written code" (Romans 2:28-29).

Adding weight to the latter view is the fact that Polycarp was martyred in Smyrna around A.D. 155. At Polycarp's trial, the unbelieving Jews of Smyrna joined with the pagans in condemning him to death. Eusebius writes that "the Jews, being especially zealous . . . ran to procure fuel" for the burning (*The Ecclesiastical History* 4:15).

After commending the church in Smyrna for their spiritual victories, Jesus warned of coming persecution: "You are about to suffer. I tell you; the devil will put some of you in prison to test you, and you will suffer persecution for ten days" (Revelation 2:10). Some of the church members would be imprisoned, and this wave of persecution would last for ten days. However, Jesus gives hope to His church: "Do not be afraid," He says. The Smyrnan Believers would have the courage to face the trial (Matthew 5:11-12).

Jesus calls them to remain faithful in their suffering: "Be faithful, even to the point of death, and I will give you the crown of life" (Revelation 2:10). Here, a specific crown is mentioned for those who die as a result of suffering for Christ. This same "martyr's crown" is also mentioned in James 1:12: "Blessed is the man who perseveres under trial, because when he has stood the test, he will receive the crown of life that God has promised to those who love him."

Jesus makes a final promise to the Believers in Smyrna: "He who overcomes will not be hurt at all by the second death" (Revelation 2:11). The overcomers, or "conquerors" identified here refers to all believers (1 John 5:4-5). The second death is a reference to the final judgment of the wicked (Revelation 20:6, 14; 21:8). Believers will not be hurt "at all" by that judgment; their sin was judged at the cross, and, in Christ, there is no more condemnation (Romans 8:1).

> Revelation 2:13-17 the church at Pergamum
> *I know where you dwell, where satan's throne is; you hold fast my name and you did not deny my faith even in the days of An'tipas my witness, my faithful one, who was killed among you, where satan dwells. But I have a few things against you: you have some there who hold the teaching of Balaam, who taught Balak to put a stumbling block before the sons of Israel, that they might eat food sacrificed to idols and practice immorality. So you also have some who hold the teaching of the Nicola'itans. Repent then. If not, I will come to you soon and war against them with the sword of my mouth. He who has an ear, let him hear what the Spirit says to the churches. To him who conquers I will give some of the hidden manna, and I will give him a white stone, with a new name written on the stone which no one knows except him who receives it.*

The message to the Pergamene church was from the Lord Jesus Christ, specifically addressed to the "angel" (or "messenger") of the church: "And to the angel of the church in Pergamum write: 'These are the words of him who has the sharp, double-edged sword'" (Revelation 2:12). This was not John's message to the Believers at Pergamum; it was a message from Jesus Christ. The depiction of Jesus holding a sharp, two-edged sword refers to the Lord's readiness to bring judgment (cf. Revelation 1:16).

First, Jesus affirms the church's positive actions: "I know where you live—where satan has his throne. Yet you remain true to my name. You did not renounce your faith in me, even in the days of Antipas, my faithful witness, who was put to death in your city—where satan lives" (Revelation 2:13). The Pergamene Believers lived in a difficult place, surrounded by pagan influences, yet they held fast to Christ's name and did not deny Him during difficult times.

One Christian in Pergamum named Antipas is mentioned as a "faithful witness." Church tradition says that Antipas was a physician suspected of secretly propagating Christianity. The Aesculapians (members of the medical guild) accused Antipas of disloyalty to Caesar. Upon being condemned to death, Antipas was placed inside a copper bull, which was then heated over a fire until it was red-hot.

The church was not perfect, however, and Jesus took note of their sin: "Nevertheless, I have a few things against you: You have people there who hold to the teaching of Balaam, who taught Balak to entice the Israelites to sin by eating food sacrificed to idols and by committing sexual immorality. Likewise, you also have those who hold to the teaching of the Nicolaitans" (Revelation 2:14-15). The "teaching of Balaam" is explained [Balaam, a Prophet from Mesopotamia, was willing to use his God-given talents for illicit purposes. Even though he knew Balak was God's enemy, he tried to sell his prophetic gifts to help him]. As Christians were eating food that had been sacrificed to idols (religious compromise) and committing sexual immorality (moral compromise). Balaam's deceitful work is described in Numbers 25:1-3 and Numbers 31:15-16. The Nicolaitans are mentioned only in this letter and in the letter to the Ephesian church (Revelation 2:6). They were likely a group similar to those who held the teachings of Balaam, though the exact nature of their doctrine and practice is unknown.

Jesus then issues a clarion call to repent of their sin: *"Repent therefore!"* (Revelation 2:16). Our Lord hates religious and moral compromise. He calls His people to live differently.

Jesus notes the judgment that would take place if the church of Pergamum did not repent: *"I will soon come to you and will fight against them with the sword of my mouth"* (Revelation 2:16b). The Nicolaitans and those who were teaching Balaam's error would be destroyed, along with their followers, from the congregation at Pergamum. Jesus desires purity among His people, and we have a responsibility to remove false teachers from the Church.

Jesus makes a final promise to the believers in Pergamum: *"To him who overcomes, I will give some of the hidden manna. I will also give him a white stone with a new name written on it, known only to him who receives it"* (Revelation 2:17). The three blessings are hidden manna, a white stone, and a new name. The precise explanation of these three items is disputed; however, all three blessings must concern the believer's victorious reign with Christ, consistent with the blessings bestowed on the other six churches of Revelation 2–3. The *"hidden manna"* is likely an allusion to the manna hidden in the Ark of the Covenant, representative of God's faithful presence and sustenance. The *"white stone"* could be a reference to the stones used for entrance into temple events in ancient times or to one of the stones on the high priest's breastplate (Exodus 28:21), although the exact meaning of the stone is uncertain.

Revelation 2:19-29 the church at Thyatira:
I know your works, your love and faith and service and patient endurance, and that your latter works exceed the first. But I have this against you, that you tolerate the woman Jez'ebel, who calls herself a prophetess and is teaching and beguiling my servants to practice immorality and to eat food sacrificed to idols. I gave her time to repent, but she refuses to repent of her immorality. Behold, I will throw her on a sickbed, and those who commit adultery with her I will throw into great tribulation, unless they repent of her doings; and I will strike her children dead. And all the churches shall know that I am he who searches mind and heart, and I will give to each of you as your works deserve. But to the rest of you in Thyati'ra, who do not hold this teaching, who have not learned what some call the deep things of satan, to you I say, I do not lay upon you any other burden; only hold fast what you have, until I come. He who conquers and who keeps my works until the end, I

will give him power over the nations, and he shall rule them with a rod of iron, as when earthen pots are broken in pieces, even as I myself have received power from my Father; and I will give him the morning star. He who has an ear, let him hear what the Spirit says to the churches.

Thyatira was a wealthy town on the Lycus River in the Roman province of Asia (modern-day Turkey).

The message was from the Lord Jesus Christ through an angel (or "messenger"): *"To the angel of the church in Thyatira write..."* (Revelation 2:18). This was not John's message to the Thyatiran Believers; it was a message from the Lord. The description at the end of verse 18 verifies the author of this message is Jesus Christ: "The words of the Son of God, whose eyes are like blazing fire and whose feet are like burnished bronze." This description removes any doubt of the identity of the One giving the message.

After identifying Himself, Jesus affirms the church's positive actions: "I know your deeds, your love and faith, your service and perseverance, and that you are now doing more than you did at first" (Revelation 2:19). Five qualities are listed:

1. love,
2. faith,
3. service,
4. patient endurance
5. greater works.

Next, Jesus notes their sin: "Nevertheless, I have this against you: You tolerate that woman Jezebel, who calls herself a prophetess. By her teaching she misleads my servants into sexual immorality and the eating of food sacrificed to idols" (Revelation 2:20). Apparently, a false prophetess was leading Believers into compromise. The church was engaging in sexual immorality and dabbling in idolatry. It is possible that "Jezebel" was her real name, but it is more likely the name was a metaphorical reference to the Jezebel of the Old Testament—another idolatrous woman who opposed God's ways. Rather than rebuke this false teacher and send her out of the church, the Believers in Thyatira were allowing her to continue her deception.

Jesus pronounces judgment on this "Jezebel" and calls the church of Thyatira to repent of their sin: *"I will cast her on a bed of suffering, and I will make those who commit adultery with her suffer intensely, unless they repent of her ways. I will strike her children dead"* (Revelation 2:22-23).

Then Jesus encourages those who had remained faithful:

Now I say to the rest of you in Thyatira, to you who do not hold to her teaching and have not learned satan's so-called deep secrets (I will not impose any other burden on you): Only hold on to what you have until I come (Revelation 2:24-25).

The faithful Believers did not fall into satan's trap, and they only needed to remain faithful until Christ's soon return.

Jesus lists His promises to the Believers in Thyatira: Revelation 2:26-28

To him who overcomes and does my will to the end, I will give authority over the nations—'He will rule them with an iron scepter; he will dash them to pieces like pottery'—just as I have received authority from my Father. I will also give him the morning star.

These blessings would include:

1. Authority over the nations,
2. Victory over all enemies, and
3. The morning star. This morning star is Jesus Himself, as Revelation 22:16 reveals. Jesus will give Himself to His church, and they will fellowship together forever.

Revelation 3:1b-6 the church at Sardis

I know your works; you have the name of being alive, and you are dead. Awake, and strengthen what remains and is on the point of death, for I have not found your works perfect in the sight of my God. Remember then what you received and heard; keep that, and repent. If you will not awake, I will come like a thief, and you will not know at what hour I will come upon you. Yet you have still a few names in Sardis, people who have not soiled their garments; and they shall walk with me in white, for they are worthy. He who conquers shall be clad thus in white garments, and I will not blot his name out of the book of life; I will confess his name before my

Father and before his angels. He who has an ear, let him hear what the Spirit says to the churches.

The message to Sardis is from the Lord Jesus Christ through an angel or messenger (possibly a reference to the Pastor):

To the angel of the church in Sardis write . . . (Revelation 3:1).

This was not John's message to the church at Sardis; it was a message from the Lord. The description at the end of verse 1 further verifies the author:

These are the words of him who holds the seven spirits of God and the seven stars. (Revelation 3:1)

Only Jesus has the seven spirits (or *"seven-fold Spirit,"* meaning the complete or perfect Spirit of God), and only Jesus holds the seven stars, i.e., the seven angels (or Pastors) of the seven churches (Revelation 1:20).

Jesus quickly and clearly condemns the lifeless state of the church at Sardis:

I know your deeds; you have a reputation of being alive, but you are dead (Revelation 3:2).

This church may have had a good reputation, but they were spiritually lifeless. In other words, the church was filled with unsaved people going through the motions of religion. There were many tares among the wheat (Matthew 13:24-30).

Jesus then calls them to repent of their sin:

Wake up! Strengthen what remains and is about to die, for I have not found your deeds complete in the sight of my God. Remember, therefore, what you received and heard; obey it, and repent (Revelation 3:2-3a).

To *"wake up"* means to start paying attention to their need of salvation, to stop being careless about their heart's condition before God.

Jesus notes the judgment that would take place if they did not repent:

If you do not wake up, I will come like a thief, and you will not know at what time I will come to you (Revelation 3:3b).

A dead church, and one unrepentant in its deadness, will be disciplined by Jesus Himself.

After the warning, Jesus encourages those in Sardis who had remained faithful:

Yet you have still a few people in Sardis who have not soiled their clothes. They will walk with me, dressed in white, for they are worthy (Revelation 3:4).

The faithful remnant had not soiled their garments (participated in sin). They are *"worthy."* The idea of walking worthily is also found in Paul's teaching in Ephesians 4:1; Colossians 1:10; and 1 Thessalonians 2:12. To be *"worthy"* is to *"match up"* with something—the profession of faith in the mouth matches the reality of faith in the heart. The faithful ones are promised to walk with Jesus in white (see Matthew 22:11-12; Revelation 19:8).

Jesus makes a final promise to the Believers in Sardis:

He who overcomes will, like them, be dressed in white. I will never blot out his name from the book of life, but will acknowledge his name before my Father and his angels (Revelation 3:5).

The one who *"overcomes"* is anyone who is born-again (1 John 5:4). The overcomer will receive a white garment (a token of righteousness), he will never have his name removed from the book of life (a promise of eternal security), and he will be confessed by Jesus in Heaven (cf. Luke 12:8).

Revelation 3:7-13 the church at Philadelphia
And to the angel of the church in Philadelphia write: 'The words of the holy one, the true one, who has the key of David, who opens and no one shall shut, who shuts and no one opens.' "I know your works.

Behold, I have set before you an open door, which no one is able to shut; I know that you have but little power, and yet you have kept my word and have not denied my name. Behold, I will make those of the synagogue of satan who say that they are Jews and are not, but lie—behold, I will make them come and bow down before your feet, and learn that I have loved you. Because you have kept my word of patient endurance, I will keep you from the hour of trial which is coming on the whole world, to try those who dwell upon the earth. I am coming soon; hold fast what you have, so that no one may seize your crown. He who conquers, I will make him a pillar in the temple of my God; never shall he go out of it, and I will write on him the name of my God, and the name of the city of my God, the new Jerusalem which comes down from my God out of heaven, and my own new name. He who has an ear, let him hear what the Spirit says to the churches.

The message is from the Lord Jesus Christ through an angel or "messenger" (likely a reference to the Pastor) in Revelation 3:7

"To the angel of the church in Philadelphia write..."

This was not John's personal message to these Believers; it was a message from the Lord, who identifies Himself as *"him who is holy and true, who holds the key of David. What he opens no one can shut, and what he shuts no one can open."* This description of Jesus emphasizes His holiness, His sovereignty, and His authority. The reference to the key of David is an allusion to the Messianic prophecy of Isaiah 22:22. Jesus is the one who opens and shuts.

Jesus affirms the church's positive actions in Revelation 3:8

I know your deeds. See, I have placed before you an open door that no one can shut. I know that you have little strength, yet you have kept my word and have not denied my name.

The church of Philadelphia was weak in some respects, yet they had remained faithful in the face of trial. Because of this, the Lord promises them an *"open door"* of blessing.

Jesus' letter then condemns the enemies of the Philadelphian Believers in

Revelation 3:9

I will make those who are of the synagogue of satan, who claim to be Jews though they are not, but are liars—I will make them come and fall down at your feet and acknowledge that I have loved you.

Those who persecuted the Believers (the persecutors were religious hypocrites in this case) would one day realize Christ loves His children. The church of Philadelphia would be victorious over its enemies.

Jesus encourages the Philadelphian Believers regarding His future coming: Revelation 3:10-11

Since you have kept my command to endure patiently, I will also keep you from the hour of trial that is going to come upon the whole world to test those who live on the earth. I am coming soon. Hold on to what you have, so that no one will take your crown.

The church's faithful endurance would serve as a blessing. Jesus would take them to be with Him before the coming tribulation (1 Thessalonians 4:13-18). He also exhorts them to remain faithful, because this would lead to rewards in the afterlife.

Jesus provides a final promise to the Believers in Philadelphia and to all Believers: Revelation 3:12

Him who overcomes I will make a pillar in the temple of my God. Never again will he leave it. I will write on him the name of my God and the name of the city of my God, the new Jerusalem, which is coming down from out of heaven from my God; and I will also write on him my new name.

Professor Thomas Constable notes, "God promised that He will not just honor overcomers by erecting a pillar in their name in Heaven, as was the custom in Philadelphia. He will make them pillars in the spiritual temple of God, the New Jerusalem (21:22; cf. Galatians 2:9; 1 Corinthians 3:16-17; 2 Corinthians 6:16; Ephesians 2:19-22; 1 Peter 2:4-10)."[21]

So, those who struggled with weakness Jesus makes everlasting pillars in the house of God. We can do all things through Christ who strengthens

---

[21] Source: Thomas Constable, Notes on Revelation at http://soniclight.org/constable/notes/pdf/revelation.pdf.

us (Philippians 4:13). Jesus' words of comfort certainly would have been a blessing to the Philadelphians who had faithfully stood for Christ in their pagan culture. His words continue to serve as an encouragement to faithful Believers today.

Revelation 3:14-21 the church at Laodicea
And to the angel of the church in La-odice a write: 'The words of the Amen, the faithful and true witness, the beginning of God's creation. "'I know your works: you are neither cold nor hot. Would that you were cold or hot! So, because you are lukewarm, and neither cold nor hot, I will spew you out of my mouth. For you say, I am rich, I have prospered, and I need nothing; not knowing that you are wretched, pitiable, poor, blind, and naked. Therefore I counsel you to buy from me gold refined by fire, that you may be rich, and white garments to clothe you and to keep the shame of your nakedness from being seen, and salve to anoint your eyes, that you may see. Those whom I love, I reprove and chasten; so be zealous and repent. Behold, I stand at the door and knock; if any one hears my voice and opens the door, I will come in to him and eat with him, and he with me. He who conquers, I will grant him to sit with me on my throne, as I myself conquered and sat down with my Father on his throne.

Laodicea was a wealthy, industrious city in the province of Phrygia in the Lycos Valley.

The message is from the Lord Jesus Christ via an angel or messenger (likely a reference to the church's Pastor) as per Revelation 3:14

To the angel of the church in Laodicea write . . .

This was not simply John's message to those in Laodicea; it was a message from the Lord. Jesus identifies Himself thus: *"The Amen, the faithful and true witness, the ruler of God's creation."* These titles emphasize the Lord's faithfulness, sovereignty, and power to bring all things to their proper completion (the *"Amen"*).

In contrast to the other six churches, the Laodicean church has nothing to be commended for. Jesus begins the message with condemnation: Revelation 3:15-17

I know your deeds, that you are neither cold nor hot. I wish you were either one or the other! So, because you are lukewarm—neither hot nor cold—I am about to spit you out of my mouth. You say, 'I am rich; I have acquired wealth and do not need a thing.' But you do not realize that you are wretched, pitiful, poor, blind and naked.

Jesus emphasizes their *"lukewarm"* apathetic nature three separate times. As a result of their ambivalence to spiritual things, Jesus would have nothing to do with them. He would *"spit them out,"* as the people of Laodicea would spit out the tepid water that flowed from the underground aqueducts to their city. With their apathy came a spiritual blindness; they claimed to be rich, blessed, and self-sufficient. Perhaps they were rich in material things. But, spiritually, the Laodiceans were in a wretched, pitiful condition, made all the worse in that they could not see their need. This was a church filled with self-deceived hypocrites.

Jesus calls the Laodicean church to repent of its sin: Revelation 3:18

I counsel you to buy from me gold refined in the fire, so you can become rich; and white clothes to wear, so you can cover your shameful nakedness; and salve to put on your eyes, so you can see.

Their material wealth had no eternal benefit, so Jesus commands them to come to Him for true, spiritual riches (see Isaiah 55:1-2). Only Christ can supply an everlasting inheritance, clothe us in righteousness, and heal our spiritual blindness.

Jesus then notes His concern for His church in Laodicea: Revelation 3:19-20

Those whom I love I rebuke and discipline. So be earnest, and repent. Here I am! I stand at the door and knock. If anyone hears my voice and opens the door, I will come in and eat with him, and he with me.

His rebuke is not born of animosity but of love. *"The Lord disciplines those he loves"* (Hebrews 12:6). The desired response to God's reproof was zealous change and true repentance.

Verse 20 is often used as an evangelistic appeal, yet its original context communicates Christ's desire for fellowship with His lukewarm church in

Laodicea. The church is nominally Christian, but Christ Himself has been locked out. Rather than turn His back on them, He knocks at the door, seeking someone to acknowledge the church's need and open the door. If they would repent, Jesus would come in and take His rightful place in the church. He would share a meal with them, a Middle Eastern word picture speaking of closeness of relationship.

Jesus then makes a promise to the Believers in Laodicea Revelation 3:21

To him who overcomes, I will give the right to sit with me on my throne, just as I overcame and sat down with my Father on his throne.

The *"overcomer"* refers to any Believer, and the promise is that he will share Christ's future Kingdom.

In summary, the church at Laodicea had become apathetic in their love for Christ. They were allowing "the deceitfulness of wealth and the desires for other things [to] come in and choke the word, making it unfruitful" (Mark 4:19). Christ called them to repent and live zealously for Him, to *"choose for yourselves this day whom you will serve"* (Joshua 24:15). The Lord Jesus issues the same call to those who say they follow Him today.

One of the issues that many face today, especially understanding the letters to the seven First Century churches as I have explained it here is that most do not think like a First Century Jew, and this is what we need to fully understand:[22]

Clearly, if you were to put yourself in the mind of a First Century Christian living in Israel, you would understand that you only have forty years to spread the gospel before Jesus comes on clouds to destroy Jerusalem and you would have to flee to the mountains. You would use language in your letters speaking of it being the last hour and the latter times, and you would say things like, He is standing at the door, and the Lord is at hand and the day is about to come. We must choose to consciously stop taking what the New Testament authors meant for those living between AD 30 and AD 70 and applying it to our future.

Many false doctrines have been created by not reading the Bible according to its historical and cultural context. Two clear examples that

---

[22] Paraphrased from Raptureless an optimistic guide to the end of the world 2nd edition copyright © 2013 Jonathan Weitem

we will look at next are the wrong expectations of an apostasy of the Church and coming false teachers.

APOSTASY
One major false teaching that currently exists is the concept of a future "fallen apostate church." Some have even tried to force Church history into seven time periods and line them up with the seven churches in Revelation chapters 2 and 3. These individuals say that the modern Church is the church of Laodicea, which Jesus threatened to vomit out of His mouth. Not only is this concept deeply incorrect, but it also contradicts everything Jesus said about His Kingdom growing (see Matthew 13:31–33). Here are some of the verses that are used to substantiate this teaching. 2 Thessalonians 2:3 KJV

Let no man deceive you by any means: for that day shall not come, except there come a falling away first, and that man of sin be revealed, the son of perdition.

This verse has been used extensively in the last fifty years to claim that the majority of the Church is not actually walking with God. Those who teach this say that the true Church is merely a remnant of those who claim to be the Church. But it is an error to drag the Old Testament remnant idea into the New Testament, where it does not belong. So, this verse should not be used to substantiate that false doctrine. Also, it is important to note that this verse is about a rebellious person called the man of sin, not about the Church falling apart. This verse is better understood in the NIV translation: 2 Thessalonians 2:3

Don't let anyone deceive you in any way, for that day will not come until the rebellion occurs and the man of lawlessness is revealed, the man doomed to destruction.

Many consider this to be speaking about the soon coming "antichrist", but this rebellion occurred in the First Century under [23] Johanan Levi. To fully understand this; here is a bit more on the antichrist:

---

[23] http://www.jewishencyclopedia.com/articles/8736-john-of-giscala-johanan-ben-levi

ANTICHRIST - (PARAPHRASED FROM JONATHAN WELTON'S BOOK RAPTURELESS)

The idea that society as we know it is heading toward complete corruption and a one-world leader has been around a long time, and many dictators have tried to make this a reality. Yet it begs this question, what does the Bible actually say about this "antichrist?" The idea of the antichrist, as it is commonly taught, comes primarily from a compilation of four different passages of Scripture. Therefore, let us examine these four passages of Scripture, with the intention to show you that there is no future one-world ruler prophesied in the Bible.

PASSAGE #1: FIRST AND SECOND JOHN

To begin, we must realize that the term antichrist does not appear in the Book of Revelation at all. A simple search of a Strong's Concordance will reveal that the term antichrist is only used in four passages in the Bible, three times in First John and once in Second John. To understand the term antichrist, we must first understand the context of John's writings.[24]

During the time of the First Century Church, there was a cult system called Gnosticism.

In the next chapter we would take a more detailed look at Gnosticism!

---

[24] [End of paraphrase of] Welton, Jonathan. Raptureless: An Optimistic Guide to the End of the World - Revised Edition Including The Art of Revelation. BookBaby. Kindle Edition.

Chapter Four
Gnosticism

THE NAME IS DERIVED FROM THE GREEK WORD "*GNOSIS*" WHICH LITERALLY MEANS *"knowledge."*

- At the foundation of First Century Gnosticism was a worldview in which the spiritual world was distinctly separated from the natural world.
- The spiritual world was considered good, and the natural world was considered corrupt.
- The leaders of this teaching/belief concluded that God could not have taken on flesh or come into this corrupt world in the form of Jesus. This led to several false teachings about the nature of Jesus.
- Thinking of this natural world as corrupt also led them to believe that a person must be very spirit-conscious to be a good Christian. Hence, they developed mystical understandings and taught that a person must have secret knowledge to know God. From this the word Gnosticism came, for it literally means "knowledge."
- During the First Century, Gnosticism took many forms, but one of the most influential Gnostic groups completely rejected the Old Testament. They declared that the God of the Old Testament was the devil and Jesus had come to reveal an "unknown Father" to us.
- Other Gnostics taught that the Old Testament rituals were still valid for Christians.

- One of the most prominent Gnostic teachers was a man called Cerinthus. He was a Jew who lived in Asia Minor, teaching that Jesus was the son of Joseph and Mary (not born of a virgin)—an ordinary man. A heavenly spirit called "the Christ" came upon Jesus at His baptism and left Him at the crucifixion. Jesus had brought secret teachings that would enable people to overcome enslavement to the physical world, but the Jewish customs also had to be observed. Those who proved faithful to these teachings and observances would live for a literal 1,000 years of sensual pleasures. These teachings of Cerinthus flourished throughout Asia Minor.
- Historical records tell us that the Apostle John was so horrified at Cerinthus' teachings that on one occasion when John walked into the public baths with his disciples at Ephesus, he saw Cerinthus and ran out of the bathhouse, warning his disciples that the house may fall down because "Cerinthus, the enemy of the truth, is inside."
- This is the setting in which Apostle John ministered. History tells us that by the year A.D. 150, one third of all Christians were under the influence of Gnosticism. It was a huge cult and a major concern of the Church fathers. John was on the front lines of that battle.

<u>Apostle John wrote to correct Gnostic Teachings as soon as we learn about the historical setting in which he ministered, we can more easily understand his writings.</u>

- For example, his Gospel starts off saying: *In the beginning was the Word, and the Word was with God, and the Word was God... And the Word became flesh, and dwelt among us, and we saw His glory.* (John 1:1-14)
- Do you see how profound this statement is? Because the Gnostics thought of the natural world as evil, they could not believe that Jesus could have been God and at the same time have taken on human flesh. John boldly told the reader that he saw Jesus. Jesus was real. Jesus came into this world. John declared that Jesus is God and Jesus took on flesh.
- John was also countering Gnosticism when he wrote his first Two Epistles. First John starts with a declaration that is diametrically opposed to the Gnostic view of Jesus. 1 John 1:1-2

> *What was from the beginning, what we have heard, what we have seen with our eyes, what we have looked at and touched with our hands, concerning the Word of Life—and the life was manifested, and we have seen and testify and proclaim to you the eternal life, which was with the Father and was manifested to us.*

Do you see how clearly and forcefully John is confronting Gnosticism? John said that he and the other Apostles heard Jesus, saw Him, and touched Him with their hands. Jesus manifested Himself in this world. He was God, and He took on flesh. This battle that John had with Gnosticism is common knowledge among Bible scholars. In fact, any student serious about understanding John's writings will be ever conscious of this fact.

First, it is important to note that certain Bible translations have inserted a word that is not in the Greek manuscripts; this has led to much confusion. These translations capitalize the word antichrist in the epistle of 1 John 2:18. The reason for the capitalization is because the translators inserted the word the before the word antichrist, thus making antichrist into a proper noun, which requires capitalization.

The Early Church had heard that antichrist (false teaching) was coming, but they had not heard that the Antichrist (a one-world ruler) was coming. The insertion of the word and the capitalization of Antichrist was added 1,500 years later by the translators. This was done because Martin Luther and the Protestants wanted to be able to point the condemning finger at the Catholic Church, therefore by making antichrist into a proper noun, they could easily identify her as being such.

With that understanding, we can discern the true meaning of John's letter. John said, *"As you have heard that antichrist is coming...."* The important question is, when had the readers of John's letter heard this message of an impending antichrist?

Considering that the term antichrist refers to Gnosticism (false teachers), it makes sense that John would be referencing what Jesus warned in Matthew 24—the coming of false teachers. The Gnosticism that John addressed in the epistles of First and Second John was the false teaching that Jesus predicted.

The verse continues, *"...even now many antichrists have come..."* (1 John 2:18). In other words, many false teachings had already come: Gnosticism, the Nicolaitan heresy, and the Judiazers' heresy (see Revelation 2:6,9,15; 3:9). John finishes this verse with, *"This is how we know it is the last hour"* (1 John 2:18). This again shows that John was referring to Jesus' prediction in Matthew 24 that one sign of the coming destruction of Jerusalem would be false teachers. So, the appearance of Gnostic heresy was a sign of it being the last hour before the destruction of Jerusalem.

John continued: 1 John 2:19 NIV

They went out from us, but they did not really belong to us. For if they had belonged to us, they would have remained with us; but their going showed that none of them belonged to us.

The Apostle John, writing before the AD 70 destruction, pointed to the fact that many had left the true Church and that this was proof that they were in the last hours of Jesus' prophecy from Matthew 24 being fulfilled. 1 John 2:20-23 NKJV

But you have been anointed by the Holy One, and you all know. I write to you, not because you do not know the truth, but because you know it, and know that no lie is of the truth. Who is the liar but **he who denies that Jesus is the Christ? This is the antichrist**, *he who denies the Father and the Son. No one who denies the Son has the Father. He who confesses the Son has the Father also.*

John writes that those who deny that Jesus is the Christ are antichrist, which is a much broader definition than one individual being a future one-world ruler. Clearly, we can see that John was writing about Gnosticism in the First Century Church. He never refers to a future one-world ruler possessed by satan himself. Antichrist does not refer to a one-world government ruler, but to ancient Gnosticism.

In the next chapter we will get back to the messages to the seven churches.

CHAPTER FIVE
A Deeper Look into the Messages to the Seven Churches - II

Let's look at our next passage.
Passage #2: Daniel 9:24-27

Seventy weeks of years are decreed concerning your people and your holy city, to finish the transgression, to put an end to sin, and to atone for iniquity, to bring in everlasting righteousness, to seal both vision and prophet, and to anoint a most holy place. Know therefore and understand that from the going forth of the word to restore and build Jerusalem to the coming of an anointed one, a prince, there shall be seven weeks. Then for sixty-two weeks it shall be built again with squares and moat, but in a troubled time. And after the sixty-two weeks, an anointed one shall be cut off, and shall have nothing; and the people of the prince who is to come shall destroy the city and the sanctuary. Its end shall come with a flood, and to the end there shall be war; desolations are decreed. And he shall make a strong covenant with many for one week; and for half of the week he shall cause sacrifice and offering to cease; and upon the wing of abominations shall come one who makes desolate, until the decreed end is poured out on the desolator.

Many modern end-times teachers use Daniel 9 to glean much of their information about the evil one-world government ruler that they believe is in our future. Yet there is no mention of an antichrist figure in Daniel 9. The commentaries written before the 1830s agree that this passage is about Jesus, not the antichrist. As the famous commentator Matthew Henry says of Daniel 9, "We have here the answer that was immediately sent to Daniel's prayer, and it is a very memorable one, as it contains *the most illustrious prediction of Christ and gospel-grace that is extant in all the Old Testament.*"[25]

But for the sake of conjecture, supposing that we believe that Daniel 9 is about a satan-possessed antichrist figure, let's look at what would need to happen in the future, according to Daniel 9. The requirements involved for this system to work are as follows:

- The Temple in Jerusalem must be rebuilt on the same exact spot as the current Dome of the Rock, which is currently a Muslim mosque.
- A functional priesthood must be reinstated.
- Animal sacrifice must be reinstituted in this rebuilt Temple.
- The prophecies regarding the "Anointed One" in Daniel 9 have to be drastically changed in order to fit the antichrist (instead of Christ).
- The antichrist must make a covenant with the whole world for three and a half years.
- The antichrist will enter the Temple and sit down as God and end animal sacrifice.

It is clear from a simple reading of Daniel 9:24–27 and a basic understanding of history that this passage has been fulfilled by Christ. There is no antichrist in Daniel 9.

Passage #3: 2 Thessalonians 2:1-8
Concerning the coming of our Lord Jesus Christ and our being gathered to him, *we ask you, brothers and sisters, not to become easily unsettled or alarmed by the teaching allegedly from us— whether by a prophecy or by word of mouth or by letter—asserting that the day of the Lord has already come* (Emphasis Author's 2 Thessalonians 2:1-2 NIV).

---

[25] Matthew Henry, *Matthew Henry Complete Commentary on the Whole Bible* 1706), Daniel 9.

In an earlier chapter (2 Thessalonians 1:5-11), we have seen that the phrase, *"the coming of our Lord Jesus Christ,"* is in reference to the destruction of Jerusalem. Also, we saw that the "gathering" mentioned here is a reference to the Christians fleeing Judea to the mountains and being gathered and protected by the Lord during the destruction of Jerusalem. From these starting points, next we will see that the Thessalonians apparently thought that the coming had already happened.

The fact that the Thessalonians could think such a thing proves that they were expecting a local event to occur in Jerusalem, not a global apocalypse. This letter to the Thessalonians was written in approximately AD 50, and Thessalonica is hundreds of miles from Jerusalem. We can see from this letter that they were under the impression that the coming of Christ had already happened, which means they thought Jerusalem had been destroyed. In response to this, Paul writes this: 2 Thessalonians 2:3 NIV

*Don't let anyone deceive you in any way, for that day will not come until **the rebellion occurs** and the man of lawlessness is revealed, the man doomed to destruction.* [Emphasis Author's]

The Apostle Paul told the Thessalonians that the destruction of Jerusalem would not come until the rebellion had occurred and the leader of the rebellion, the "man of lawlessness," was revealed. He then told them what types of things this rebel leader would do.

2 Thessalonians 2:4 NIV
He will oppose and will exalt himself over everything that is called God or is worshiped, so that he sets himself up in God's temple, proclaiming himself to be God.

This is a clear indicator of who could and could not be the "man of sin." For example, this would have to be a person who would have physically been able to stand in the Temple and proclaim himself God. This would require a person who was living before AD 70, when the Temple was destroyed, because at no time since AD 70 has there been a Temple for the man of sin to stand in. Also, there is no New Testament verse, not even one, that predicts a rebuilt Jewish Temple. So, the Temple had to be standing for the man of lawlessness to stand in it.

When we read in Chapter 3 about the destruction of Jerusalem, we met a few characters involved in that story. The main rebel who caused the destruction of Jerusalem was John Levi of Gischala. I believe that he clearly fits the description of the man of lawlessness in this passage.

The Jewish historian Josephus wrote of how John Levi was a selfish, unscrupulous man with persuasive powers who convinced many that he was sent by God to liberate them. Further, John Levi took over the Temple, set himself up in the Temple as the Jewish Saviour (as God), looted the vessels of the Temple for their gold, and caused the daily animal sacrifices to cease. He also plundered the people, even burning their storehouses of food and causing the great famine that starved tens of thousands to death, and he enlisted aid from the Idumeans, who killed 8,500 of the Jews, including the priests. (Second Thessalonians 2:9 speaks of counterfeit signs, the main one being that John Levi declared that he was God and would deliver the people from the Romans. He commanded the storehouses of food to be burned in faith that God would miraculously deliver them from their enemies. Instead, they starved to death.)

Even when the Roman General Titus pleaded that John Levi leave the Temple, so that it wouldn't be destroyed in battle, John flatly refused. John Levi caused the Temple to be destroyed; without him, the Temple might have been spared, considering that it was one of the wonders of the ancient world.[26]

Paul goes on to explain more about the man of lawlessness: 2 Thessalonians 2:5-7 NIV

Do you not remember that when I was still with you I told you this? And you know what is restraining him now so that he may be revealed in his time. For the mystery of lawlessness is already at work; only he who now restrains it will do so until he is out of the way.

John was not only a rebel leader, but also a false messiah. He claimed godhood by taking over the Temple, and the only person who stood in his way was the Jewish Chief Priest, Ananus. Ananus had tremendous diplomatic skills and had been able to negotiate peace treaties with Rome

---

[26] Information about John Levi in this section is gathered from *The Man of Sin of 2 Thessalonians 2* by John L Bray (Lakeland FL: L. Bray Ministry, 1997).

many times before. Ananus was literally able to restrain the full-scale rebellion that John Levi was aiming to accomplish.[27] That is why Paul referred to the one who restrained, who must be taken out of the way.

Even Josephus noted that once Ananus (the one who restrains) was killed, then the destruction of Jerusalem began:

I should not mistake if I said that the death of Ananus was the beginning of the destruction of the city, and that from this very day may be dated the overthrow of her wall, and the ruin of her affairs.[28]

As Josephus recorded, this happened exactly as the Apostle Paul laid out for the Thessalonians: 2 Thessalonians 2:8 NIV

And then the lawless one will be revealed, whom the Lord Jesus will overthrow with the breath of his mouth and destroy by the splendor of his coming.

When the "coming of the Lord" occurred with the destruction of Jerusalem, John Levi was finally dealt with. He was the cause of the rebellion, which led to the attack by the Romans. John was a deceiver who declared *"lying signs and wonders"* (2 Thessalonians 2:9–12) and caused the people to burn all the storehouses of food, claiming he was God and would provide for them! Then he set up his militia in the Temple, murdered all the priests, and caused not only all of Jerusalem to be destroyed, but even the Temple, which the Romans didn't want to harm. John Levi was so evil it boggles the mind!

A Final Thought When we think about this passage from the perspective of its original recipients, it does not make sense that Paul would have written a mysterious passage that would be of no value to his original readers and would have no value until 2,000 years in the future. The "secret power of iniquity" was already in operation in the first century; this culminated in the AD 70 judgment of iniquity (see 2 Thessalonians 2:7).

The "secret power of iniquity" hasn't been in operation for 2,000 years waiting for our future. Instead, Paul was clearly talking about an evil person in the first century and another person who was restraining this evil. John Levi and Ananus fulfill this passage.

---

[27] *Ibid.*
[28] Josephus, *The Jewish War, 313.*

PASSAGE #4: THE BEAST OF REVELATION 13 AND 17

Revelation 13 speaks of the beast, which the majority of Church history has taught represents the Roman Empire of the first century. As F.W. Farrar wrote in 1882:

Every Jewish reader, of course, saw that the beast was a symbol of Nero. And both Jews and Christians regarded Nero as also having close affinities with the serpent or dragon. . . .. All the earliest Christian writers on the Apocalypse, from Irenaeus down to Victorinus of Pettau and Commodian in the fourth, and Andreas in the Fifth, and St. Beatus in the eighth century, connect Nero, or some Roman Emperor, with the Apocalyptic beast.[29]

Revelation 17 speaks of another beast, which Church history has taught also represents the Roman Emperor Nero. I agree that these are both excellent and sensible explanations.

Revelation 17:10—The Emperor Nero
They are also seven kings.

Revelation 17:10 NIV
Five have fallen, one is, the other has not yet come; *but when he does come, he must remain for only a little while.* [Emphasis Author's]

This passage, which is speaking of the line of rulers in Rome, tells us exactly how many rulers had already come, which one was currently in power, and that the next one would only last a short while. Take a look at how that perfectly fits with Nero and the Roman Empire of the First Century. The rule of the first seven Roman Emperors are as follows:

1. Julius Caesar (49–44 BC)
2. Augustus (27 BC–AD 14)
3. Tiberius (AD 14–37)
4. Caligula (AD 37–41)
5. Claudius (AD 41–54)

"Five have fallen..."

---

[29] FW Farrah, *The Early Days of Christianity*, 471-472.

Chapter Five: A Deeper Look into the Messages to the Seven Churches - II

6. Nero (AD 54–68)

"One is..."

7. Galba (June AD 68–January AD 69, a six-month rulership) "the other has not yet come; but when he does come, he must remain for only a little while."

Of the first seven kings of the Roman Empire, five had come (Julius Caesar, Augustus, Tiberius, Gaius, and Claudius), one was now in power (Nero), and one had not yet come (Galba), but would only remain a little time (six months). The vast majority throughout Church history have understood that the beast in Revelation 17 is a reference to Nero.

> Revelation 13:1-4 NIV—The Roman Empire
> *...And I saw a beast coming out of the sea. It had...seven heads.... One of the heads of the beast seemed to have had a fatal wound, but the fatal wound had been healed. The whole world was filled with wonder and followed the beast. People worshiped the dragon because he had given authority to the beast, and they also worshiped the beast and asked, "Who is like the beast? Who can wage war against it?*

We have just seen from Revelation 17 that Nero fits the timeline as the sixth of the seven heads and that Galba *is the one to come that shall only remain a little while.* I would propose that Rome was metaphorically wounded and faltering as an empire because of Nero. Nero was not only a psychopath who burned down one third of Rome and pinned the blame on the Christians and persecuted them brutally, but also, when Nero killed himself (in AD 68), the political climate of Rome changed dramatically. One of the major changes was that Nero was officially the last of the Julio-Claudian line of emperors; thus, the line ended, and it would have seemed, symbolically, as if the head of the empire had been wounded to death.

Nero's sudden death caused an event that has been historically called the "Year of the Four Emperors." Because of tumult caused by his suicide, three short-lived emperors followed Nero. Many thought that the Roman Empire was about to die.[30]

Here is the timeline of AD 69, the "Year of the Four Emperors":

- Nero (AD 54–68)
- Galba (AD 68–69)
- Otho (AD 69)
- Vitellius (AD 69)
- Vespasian (AD 69–80)

Can you imagine if the United States had four presidents in office in a one-year period? This was a very painful year for Rome, and many thought the beast of the Roman Empire had been wounded unto death. In fact, this was the most tumultuous time in Roman history since Mark Antony's death in 30 BC, nearly 100 years earlier.

Yet, by what appeared to be a miraculous turn around, the Empire was revived under Vespasian and Titus. When they came into power, they established the Flavian dynasty of Caesars. Instead of the beast dying, it resurrected under Vespasian, and he ruled for a solid ten years.

Often this subject of the beast is connected in people's minds with the infamous "mark of the beast" found in Revelation 13:16–17. This "mark of the beast" has been the cause of much fear, so I will address it here. Regarding the "mark of the beast," it is important to note that in the ancient culture of Rome, the public market was the main source of trade and retail. For people to enter the public market, they had to pass through the main gate. It was required of all who entered the main gate to pay homage to the idol of the Emperor. Once homage was paid, ashes were placed on the hand or on the forehead of the individual, and then they were allowed to pass through the gates and buy and sell merchandise.[31] This was taking the mark. The parallels between this and the "mark of the beast" are stunning, and they further confirm the reality that the beast was Nero and the Roman Empire.

The prestigious N.T. Wright writes regarding this:

---

[30] "Emperor Nero," *The Preterist Archive;* http://preteristarchive.com/Rome/Monarchs/Nero.html.
[31] "Revelation 13:18: Number of the Beast," *The Preterist Archive;* http://preteristarchive.com/BibleStudies/ApocalypseCommentaries/revelation_13-18.html.

What's more, worshipping or nor worshipping was quickly becoming the dividing line between people who were acceptable in the community and people who weren't. Not long after this time, some local officials introduced a formal requirement that unless you had offered the required sacrifices you weren't allowed in the market. There were various kinds of marks and visible signs, which were used to set people apart either as 'able to trade' or as 'not able to trade'. From quite early on the Christians were faced with a stark alternative: stay true to the lamb and risk losing your livelihood, the ability to sell or buy; capitulate to the monster, sacrifice to Caesar at the behest of the local officials, and then everything will be all right-except your integrity as one of the lamb's followers.[32]

Another author adds:

The Christians of the First Century were under the military authority of Rome, a nation which openly proclaimed its rulers, the Caesars, to be divine. All those under the jurisdiction of Rome were required by law to publicly proclaim their allegiance to Caesar by burning a pinch of incense and declaring, "Caesar is Lord." Upon compliance with this law, the people were given a papyrus document called a "libellus," which they were required to present when either stopped by the Roman police or attempting to engage in commerce in the Roman marketplace, increasing the difficulty of "buying or selling" without this mark. This is the essence of Scripture's warnings to the early Christians against taking upon themselves the "mark of the beast."[33]

Many ancient sources spoke of Nero as a beast, as R.C. Sproul shows in his book, The Last Days According to Jesus:

[Kenneth] Gentry gives a synopsis of Nero's violence-studded life, including the murders of his own family members, the castration

---

[32] N. T. Wright, *Revelation for Everyone* (Louisville, KY: Westminster John Knox Press, 2011), 121.
[33] Richard Anthony, "The Mark of the Beast," *Ecclesia.org;* www.ecclesia.org/truth/beast.html.

of a boy Nero "married," and the brutal murder of his pregnant wife by kicking her to death. Bizarre behavior was noted by the historian Suetonius, who wrote that Nero even "devised a kind of game, in which, covered with the skin of some wild animal, he was let loose from a cage and attacked the private parts of men and women, who were bound to stakes."

Nero began his reign as emperor in A.D. 54. His imperial persecution of the Christian community was launched in A.D. 64, the same year as the famous fire (which burned 1/3 of Rome) that many believe was set by Nero himself. It is often assumed that the persecution of Christians, whom Nero blamed for the fire, was a diversionary tactic to shift blame for his own actions to others. Nero committed suicide in A.D. 68, when he was but 31 years of age.

Since the beast's appearance is one of the "things, which must shortly take place" (Revelation 1:1), Nero is at least a prima facie candidate for the role of the beast. As described by ancient historians, Nero is a singularly cruel and unrestrained man of evil. Many ancient writers cite the bestial character of Nero, and Gentry summarizes these references:

Tacitus...spoke of Nero's "cruel nature" that "put to death so many innocent men." Roman naturalist Pliny the Elder... described Nero as "the destroyer of the human race" and "the poison of the world." Roman satirist Juvenal...speaks of "Nero's cruel and bloody tyranny." ...Apollonius of Tyana... specifically mentions that Nero was called a "beast": "In my travels, which have been wider than ever man yet accomplished, I have seen many, many wild beasts of Arabia and India; but this beast, that is commonly called a Tyrant, I know not how many heads it has, nor if it be crooked of claw, and armed with horrible fangs... And of wild beasts you cannot say that they were ever known to eat their own mother, but Nero has gorged himself on this diet."[34]

The beast is not a coming antichrist or the man of lawlessness. The beast was Nero and the Roman Empire. It is amazing how perfectly the visions of John fit with what has taken place in the past!

What we need to understand:

---

[34] R. C. Sprout, *The Last Days According to Jesus* (Grand Rapids, MI: Baker Books, 1998), 186-187.

- The antichrist is not and never was a person; it is a spiritual system of false teaching, specifically Gnosticism.
- Jesus is the perfect and sensible fulfillment of Daniel 9; there is no antichrist in this passage.
- The man of lawlessness was a First Century individual; the restrainer was another First Century individual—specifically John Levi and the High Priest Ananus.
- The beast of Revelation is the Roman Empire, especially under Nero Caesar.
- There is nothing in the Bible that points to a future one-world government ruler such as has been popularized in the last century.[35]

Let us briefly go back to an earlier passage of Scripture: 2 Thessalonians 2:3 KJV

Let no man deceive you by any means: for that day shall not come, except there come a falling away first, and that man of sin be revealed, the son of perdition.

Again, we need to remind ourselves that we are reading a passage of Scripture written to the Early Church over 2,000 years ago. So, we need to capture the sense of what the Spirit of the Lord is saying. As we read this passage, we cannot read it believing that it is speaking to us here in the 21st Century.

So, we are not looking for a future "falling away" to fulfill this passage.

FALSE TEACHERS

Similar to the idea of the apostate Church is the belief that there will be many false teachers before the return of Christ. This has created a great excuse for finger-pointing in the Body of Christ and empowers a suspicious and fearful attitude toward others. As you may guess, however, the verses that are used to support this teaching were, in fact, referring to the time leading up to AD 70, not to our own day. For example: 2 Timothy 4:3-4 NIV

For the time will come when people will not put up with sound doctrine. Instead, to suit their own desires, they will gather around

---

[35] [End of paraphrased] Welton, Jonathan. Raptureless: An Optimistic Guide to the End of the World - Revised Edition Including The Art of Revelation. BookBaby. Kindle Edition.

them a great number of teachers to say what their itching ears want to hear. They will turn their ears away from the truth and turn aside to myths.

The *"sound doctrine"* would have been that judgment was coming to Jerusalem, but the *"itching ears"* wanted to hear from false prophets and teachers that declared God's protection from destruction. This provided a stage for a major rise in false prophets and teachers between AD 30 and AD 70. Now look at this verse: 1 Timothy 4:1 NKJV

Now the Spirit expressly says that in latter times some will depart from the faith, giving heed to deceiving spirits and doctrines of demons.

These latter times referred to by Paul were not 2,000 years later. This was in reference to the false teachers and false prophets of the First Century (the same is true of Second Timothy 3). We must choose to interpret Scripture correctly and not pull verses out of their intended context to fit our personal agenda. Here is another passage that many have misunderstood: Amos 8:11 NIV

"The days are coming," declares the Sovereign LORD, "when I will send a famine through the land—not a famine of food or a thirst for water, but a famine of hearing the words of the LORD".

This is not a New Testament prophecy. This was fulfilled by the 400 years between the end of the Old Testament and the start of the New Testament, where there is no recorded spoken word from God. Now look at these two passages, the first from the Apostle Paul and the second from Jesus: Acts 20:29-31 NIV

I know that after I leave, [not 2,000 years later] savage wolves will come in among you and will not spare the flock. Even from your own number men will arise and distort the truth in order to draw away disciples after them. So be on your guard! Remember that for three years I never stopped warning each of you night and day with tears.

> *And will not God bring about justice for his chosen ones, who cry out to him day and night? Will he keep putting them off? I tell you, he will see that they get justice, and quickly. However, when the Son of Man comes, will he find faith on the earth?* (Luke 18:7-8 NIV)

Will He keep putting them off? No, Jesus will not. He will see that they get justice quickly. Remember that the word comes is a reference to the First Century destruction of Jerusalem, not to events 2,000 years later. This was perfectly fulfilled; they got justice and quickly!

We need to fully understand the following:

- There is no separation in the three questions that the disciples asked Jesus as recorded in Matthew 24:3. There is no separation in the answers that Jesus gave His disciples.
- When the New Testament mentions the end of the age, it is referring to the end of the Age of Moses, not the end of the world.
- The idea of the seven churches of Revelation corresponding with seven periods in Church history has no foundation.
- The Kingdom of God is growing, and we are not looking for a future "falling away" of the Church.
- The passages that speak of false teachers, teachings, and prophets were all fulfilled in the First Century. These have no prophetic significance for the modern day, although they have practical significance. We still need to use discernment regarding teaching and judge the fruit, but we are not looking for a future apostasy.

In the next chapter we would like to look at The Seven Seals and their meaning.

CHAPTER SIX
THE SEVEN SEALS

As we seen thus far, in Revelation chapter 1, John meets Jesus on the island of Patmos. Then in Revelation 2–3, Jesus gave letters to John for seven literal churches in the First Century while at the same time giving him a metaphoric overview of Israel's history from Genesis to the First Century nation of Israel that was about to be vomited out of the land. So, now we are going to dig a bit deeper into this book of prophecy and examine some of the more challenging components. Most scholars interpret chapters 4 and 5 similarly. In Revelation 4 and 5, we find God the Father enthroned in Heaven similarly to the visions of Isaiah 6 and Ezekiel 1. A scroll of judgement is brought forth and there is no one that can open it. That was until Jesus, as the Lamb slain, appears and begins to open the scroll of judgment.

I believe that this proves to the reader that judgment was not to be poured out until after the New Covenant had been ratified by Jesus' death on the cross and His ascension into Heaven. Most scholars agree Revelation 6–8 is a parallel of Matthew 24, although they debate the timing of Matthew 24's fulfillment.

Let us now take a brief look at the major components of these chapters and how they parallel Matthew 24:

From the individual letters to the seven churches the Revelation then moves on to the seven seals: It begins with John being caught up into Heaven, into God's Throne room: Revelation 4:1-6

After this I looked, and lo, in heaven an open door! And the first voice, which I had heard speaking to me like a trumpet, said, "Come up hither, and I will show you what must take place after this." At once I was in the Spirit, and lo, a throne stood in heaven, with one seated on the throne! And he who sat there appeared like jasper and carnelian, and round the throne was a rainbow that looked like an emerald. Round the throne were twenty-four thrones, and seated on the thrones were twenty-four elders, clad in white garments, with golden crowns upon their heads. From the throne issue flashes of lightning, and voices and peals of thunder, and before the throne burn seven torches of fire, which are the seven spirits of God; and before the throne there is as it were a sea of glass, like crystal. And round the throne, on each side of the throne, are four living creatures, full of eyes in front and behind:

The first seal Christ opens reveals the first horseman of the apocalypse. The first four seals reveal a total of *four* horsemen.

Revelation 6:1-2
Now I saw when the Lamb opened one of the seven seals, and I heard one of the four living creatures say, as with a voice of thunder, "Come!" ² And I saw, and behold, a white horse, and its rider had a bow; and a crown was given to him, and he went out conquering and to conquer.

These seals have a very similar ring to what is recorded in Matthew chapter 24. Again, remember we are looking at the last book of the Holy writings dated prior to the fall of Jerusalem of AD 70. This Revelation has nothing to do with us living some 2,000 years later and must not be interpreted that way. We must go back to the First Century Jewish era to fully grasp and understand what was being communicated.

Jonathan Welton in his book Raptureless describes these seals very well. I would like to paraphrase him here, and have obtained permission to do so:

SEAL 1: HORSEMAN 1
The first seal and horseman symbolize conquest, a parallel to *"nation rising against nation"* in Matthew 24:7. This refers to the fragmenting of the Pax Romana (Roman Peace) of the First Century.

SEAL 2: HORSEMAN 2
The first seal and horseman clearly lead to the second seal and horseman, which symbolize the *"wars and rumors of war"* in Matthew 24:6.

SEAL 3: HORSEMAN 3
The third seal and horseman clearly symbolize famine, mirroring Matthew 24:7's prophecy of the widespread First Century famines. Interestingly, in this picture, John hears this detail: *Then I heard what sounded like a voice among the four living creatures, saying, "Two pounds of wheat for a day's wages, and six pounds of barley for a day's wages, and do not damage the oil and the wine"* (Revelation 6:6). According to Robert Mounce, this means the price had risen 1,000 percent from its former price. Josephus recorded much regarding the unbelievable famine that occurred in AD 67–70.[36] From his records, we know this famine lived up to these awful predictions.

SEAL 4: HORSEMAN 4
The fourth seal and horseman symbolize the sword, plagues, famine, and death—the natural outcomes caused by the first three horsemen of conquest, war, and famine.

SEAL 5: MARTYRS
The fifth seal gives a picture of martyrs crying out to God for judgment. These are the Christians who were persecuted and martyred during AD 30–70. In this vision, they cry out to God, *"How much longer?"* The implication in the First Century (as we have already discussed) was "How much longer until the AD 70 destruction occurs?" They were calling for God's judgment against the Old Covenant and the apostate nation of Israel, not for Jesus' final return. They reappear in their white garments in the sixth seal.

---

[36] Robert Mounce, *The Book of Revelation* (Grand Rapids, MI; Eerdmans, 1977), 155.

SEAL 6: AN EARTHQUAKE, THE HEAVENS SHAKEN, THE 144,000 SEALED, AND THE GREAT MULTITUDE IN WHITE ROBES

The sixth seal contains several events that together symbolize the destruction of Jerusalem in AD 70.

First, an earthquake shakes the heavens and the earth. This parallels Matthew 24:7, 29.

> *For nation will rise against nation, and kingdom against kingdom, and there will be famines and earthquakes in various places: ... Immediately after the tribulation of those days the sun will be darkened, and the moon will not give its light, and the stars will fall from heaven, and the powers of the heavens will be shaken;*

Second, the 144,000 are sealed. This number symbolizes wholeness and represents the entire First Century Christian community, which followed Jesus' instructions in Matthew 24:15–21 by fleeing to the nearby mountains of Pella. As a result, not one Christian died in the destruction of AD 70. (This also parallels Ezekiel 9.)

Third, we get another glimpse of the martyred Saints, this time post-judgment. Since the sixth seal pictures the destruction of Jerusalem, with the shaking of the heavens and earth and the 144,000 (the entire Christian community at that point) fleeing to Mount Pella for protection, we know this group in white robes is the same as the group in the fifth seal. Now they are pictured after their pleas for justice have been fulfilled in the AD 70 destruction.

SEAL 7: SILENCE FOR THIRTY MINUTES

This symbolizes the rest that came after the AD 70 destruction. In fact, this is the quietest period in Church history. Very little is recorded about the period directly following the destruction of Jerusalem. The persecution of the Church by the Jewish Temple leaders completely halted, and the Church enjoyed a short period of peace at Mount Pella, which the seventh seal depicts as silence. [End of paraphrase].

After the seven seals we get to the seven trumpets, which begin in Revelation 8:7

The Seven Trumpets of Revelation announce that this judgement is about to be poured out upon Israel for her rejection of Jesus Christ.

Throughout this section flies the Eagle-cherub with his cry of Woe, a reminder of the conquering nation warned of in Deuteronomy 28:49. The Eagle is a Biblical symbol of both Covenant blessing (cf. Exodus 19:4; Deuteronomy 32:11) and Covenant curse (cf. Jeremiah 4:13; Habakkuk 1:8). Like the opening of Hosea's Sanctions/ Covenant Ratification section (Hosea 8:1), the Eagle in Revelation is connected with the blowing of Trumpets signalling disaster; yet the Eagle brings salvation as well to the faithful of the covenant (cf Revelation 12:14).

The First Trumpet Revelation 8:6-7
Now the seven angels who had the seven trumpets made ready to blow them. Now the seven angels who had the seven trumpets made ready to blow them. The first angel blew his trumpet, and there followed hail and fire, mixed with blood, which fell on the earth; and a third of the earth was burnt up, and a third of the trees were burnt up, and all green grass was burnt up.

We need to be reminded of the fall of Jericho, as we read about these judgements brought about by the sounding of these trumpets. They are also reminiscent of the plagues that came upon Egypt prior to the Exodus. Together, they are represented as destroying one third of the Land. Obviously, since the judgment is neither total nor final, it cannot be the end of the physical world. Nevertheless, the devastation is tremendous, and does work to bring about the end of the Jewish nation, the subject of these terrible prophecies. Israel has become a nation of Egyptians and Canaanites, and worse: a land of covenant apostates. All the curses of the Law are about to be poured out upon those who had once been the people of God (Matthew 23:35-36). The first four trumpets apparently refer to the series of disasters that devastated Israel in the "Last Days", [between AD 30-70] occurred and primarily the events leading up to the outbreak of war and the destruction of the Temple.

The Second Trumpet Revelation 8:8-9
The second angel blew his trumpet, and something like a great mountain, burning with fire, was thrown into the sea; and a third of the sea became blood, a third of the living creatures in the sea died, and a third of the ships were destroyed.

With the trumpet blast of the second angel, we see a parallel to the first plague on Egypt, in which the Nile was turned to blood and the fish died (Exodus 7:17-20. The cause of this calamity was that a great mountain burning with fire was cast into the sea. The meaning of this becomes clear when we remember that the nation of Israel was God's "Holy Mountain," the "mountain of God's inheritance" (Exodus 15:17 *You will bring them in and plant them In the mountain of Your inheritance, In the place, O Lord, which You have made For Your own dwelling, The sanctuary, O Lord, which Your hands have established.*). As the redeemed people of God, they had been brought back to Eden, and the repeated use of mountain-imagery throughout their history (including the fact that Mount Zion was the accepted symbol of the nation) demonstrates this vividly. But now, as apostates, Israel had become a "destroying mountain," against whom God's wrath had turned. God is now speaking of *Jerusalem* in the same language He once used to speak of *Babylon*.

The Third Trumpet Revelation 8:10-11
The third angel blew his trumpet, and a great star fell from heaven, blazing like a torch, and it fell on a third of the rivers and on the fountains of water. The name of the star is Wormwood. A third of the waters became wormwood, and many men died of the water, because it was made bitter.

Like the preceding symbol, the vision of the Third Trumpet combines Biblical imagery from the fall of both Egypt and Babylon. The effect of this plague - the waters being made bitter-is similar to the first plague on Egypt, in which the water became bitter because of the multitude of dead and decaying fish (Exodus 7:21 NKJV *The fish that were in the river died, the river stank, and the Egyptians could not drink the water of the river. So there was blood throughout all the land of Egypt.*). The bitterness of the waters is caused by a great star that fell from heaven, burning like a torch. This parallels Isaiah's prophecy of the fall of Babylon, spoken in terms of the original Fall from Paradise:

Isaiah 14:12-15
How you are fallen from heaven, O Day Star, son of Dawn! How you are cut down to the ground, you who laid the nations low! You said

in your heart, 'I will ascend to heaven; above the stars of God I will set my throne on high; I will sit on the mount of assembly in the far north; I will ascend above the heights of the clouds, I will make myself like the Most High.' But you are brought down to Sheol, to the depths of the Pit.

The name of this fallen star is Wormwood, a term used in the Law and the Prophets to warn Israel of its destruction as a punishment for apostasy (Deuteronomy 29:18; Jeremiah 9:15; 23:15; Lamentations 3:15, 19; Amos 5:7). Again, by combining these Old Testament allusions, John makes his point: Israel is apostate and has become an Egypt; Jerusalem has become a Babylon; and the covenant-breakers will be destroyed, as surely as Egypt and Babylon were destroyed.

The Fourth Trumpet Revelation 8:12
The fourth angel blew his trumpet, and a third of the sun was struck, and a third of the moon, and a third of the stars, so that a third of their light was darkened; a third of the day was kept from shining, and likewise a third of the night. Then I looked, and I heard an eagle crying with a loud voice, as it flew in midheaven, "Woe, woe, woe to those who dwell on the earth, at the blasts of the other trumpets which the three angels are about to blow!"

Like the ninth Egyptian plague of "thick darkness" (Exodus 10:21-23), the curse brought by the fourth angel strikes the light-bearers, the sun, moon, and stars, so that a third of them might be darkened. The imagery here was long used in the Prophets to depict the fall of nations and national rulers (cf. Isaiah 13:9-11, 19; 24:19-23; 34:4-5; Ezekiel 32:7-8, 11-12; Joel 2:10, 28-32; Acts 2:16-20. In fulfillment of this, Farrar observes, "ruler after ruler, chieftain after chieftain of the Roman Empire and the Jewish nation was assassinated and ruined. Gaius, Claudius, Nero, Galba, Otho, Vitellius, all died by murder or suicide; Herod the Great, Herod Antipas, Herod Agrippa, and most of the Herodian Princes, together with not a few of the leading High Priests of Jerusalem, perished in disgrace, or in exile, or by violent hands. All these were quenched suns and darkened stars."[37]

---

[37] F. W. Farrar, *The Early Days of Christianity* (Chicago: Belford. Clarke and Co., Publishers, 1882). p. 519.

The Fifth Trumpet – Revelation 9:1-12

And the fifth angel blew his trumpet, and I saw a star fallen from heaven to earth, and he was given the key of the shaft of the bottomless pit; he opened the shaft of the bottomless pit, and from the shaft rose smoke like the smoke of a great furnace, and the sun and the air were darkened with the smoke from the shaft. Then from the smoke came locusts on the earth, and they were given power like the power of scorpions of the earth; they were told not to harm the grass of the earth or any green growth or any tree, but only those of mankind who have not the seal of God upon their foreheads; they were allowed to torture them for five months, but not to kill them, and their torture was like the torture of a scorpion, when it stings a man. And in those days men will seek death and will not find it; they will long to die, and death will fly from them. In appearance the locusts were like horses arrayed for battle; on their heads were what looked like crowns of gold; their faces were like human faces, their hair like women's hair, and their teeth like lions' teeth; they had scales like iron breastplates, and the noise of their wings was like the noise of many chariots with horses rushing into battle. They have tails like scorpions, and stings, and their power of hurting men for five months lies in their tails. They have as king over them the angel of the bottomless pit; his name in Hebrew is Abad'don, and in Greek he is called Apol'lyon. The first woe has passed; behold, two woes are still to come.

With the first woe, the plagues become more intense. While this curse is similar to the great swarms of locusts which came upon Egypt in the eighth plague (Ex. 10:12-15), these "locusts" are different: they are *demons* from the Abyss, the bottomless pit, spoken of seven times in Revelation (9:1, 2, 11; 11:7; 17:8; 20:1, 3). The Septuagint first uses the term in Genesis 1:2, speaking of the original deep-and-darkness which the Spirit creatively overshadowed (and metaphorically "overcame"; cf. John 1:5). The Abyss is the farthest extreme from heaven (Genesis 49:25; Deuteronomy 33:13) and from the high mountains (Psalms 36:6). It is used in Scripture as a reference to the deepest parts of the sea (Job 28:14; 38:16; Psalms 33:7) and to subterranean rivers and vaults of water (Deuteronomy 8:7; Job 38:16), whence the waters of the Flood came (Genesis 7:11; 8:2), and which nourished the kingdom of Assyria (Ezekiel 31:4, 15).

The Sixth Trumpet Revelation 9:13-16

Then the sixth angel blew his trumpet, and I heard a voice from the four horns of the golden altar before God, saying to the sixth angel who had the trumpet, "Release the four angels who are bound at the great river Euphra'tes." So the four angels were released, who had been held ready for the hour, the day, the month, and the year, to kill a third of mankind. The number of the troops of cavalry was twice ten thousand times ten thousand; I heard their number. And this was how I saw the horses in my vision: the riders wore breastplates the color of fire and of sapphire and of sulphur, and the heads of the horses were like lions' heads, and fire and smoke and sulphur issued from their mouths. By these three plagues a third of mankind was killed, by the fire and smoke and sulphur issuing from their mouths. For the power of the horses is in their mouths and in their tails; their tails are like serpents, with heads, and by means of them they wound. The rest of mankind, who were not killed by these plagues, did not repent of the works of their hands nor give up worshiping demons and idols of gold and silver and bronze and stone and wood, which cannot either see or hear or walk; nor did they repent of their murders or their sorceries or their immorality or their thefts.

Again, we are reminded that the desolations wrought by God in the earth are on behalf of His people (Psalms 46), in response to their official, covenantal worship: the command to the sixth angel is issued by a voice from the four horns of the golden altar (i.e., the incense altar) which is before God. The mention of this point is obviously intended to encourage God's people in worship and prayer, assuring them that God's actions in history proceed from his altar, where He has received their prayers.

The Seventh Trumpet Revelation 11:15-19

Then the seventh angel blew his trumpet, and there were loud voices in heaven, saying, "The kingdom of the world has become the kingdom of our Lord and of his Christ, and he shall reign for ever and ever." And the twenty-four elders who sit on their thrones before God fell on their faces and worshiped God, saying, "We give thanks to thee, Lord God Almighty, who art and who wast, that thou hast taken thy great power and begun to reign. The nations raged, but thy wrath came, and the time for the dead to be judged, for rewarding thy servants, the prophets and saints, and those who fear thy name, both small and great, and for destroying the destroyers of the earth." Then God's temple in heaven was opened, and the ark of his covenant was seen within his temple; and there were flashes of lightning, voices, peals of thunder, an earthquake, and heavy hail.

In conformity with the Biblical pattern uniting the ideas of sabbath and consummation, the Trumpet of the seventh angel announces that "the Mystery of God" has been fulfilled and accomplished (cf. 10:6-7). At this point in history God's plan is made apparent: He has placed Jews and Gentiles on equal footing in the Covenant. The destruction of apostate Israel and the Temple revealed that God had created a new nation, a new Temple, as Jesus had prophesied to the Jewish leaders: *"Therefore I tell you, the kingdom of God will be taken away from you and given to a nation producing the fruits of it."* (Matthew 21:43).

Later, Jesus told His disciples what the effect of the destruction of Jerusalem would be: *"then will appear the sign of the Son of man in heaven, and then all the tribes of the earth will mourn, and they will see the Son of man coming on the clouds of heaven with power and great glory;"* (Matthew 24:30). Marcellus Kik explains: "The judgment upon Jerusalem was the sign of the fact that the Son of man was reigning in heaven. There has been misunderstanding due to the reading of this verse, as some have thought it" to be 'a sign in heaven.' But this is not what the verse says; it says the sign of the *Son of Man in heaven.* The phrase 'in heaven' defines the locality of the Son of Man and not of the sign. A sign was not to appear in the heavens, but the destruction of Jerusalem was to indicate the rule of the Son of Man in heaven."[38]

---

[38] Marcellus Kik, *An Eschatology of Victory* (Nutley, NJ: The Presbyter- ian and Reformed Publishing Co., 1970, p. 137. The common rendering in modern versions of the Bible ("then the sign of the Son of Man will appear in the sky") simply reflects the unbiblical biases of a few translators and editors. The more literal translation in the King James Version is what the Greek text *says.* Cf. the discussion in *Paradise Restored: A Biblical Theology of Dominion* (Ft. Worth, TX: Dominion Press, 1985), pp. 97-105.

Kik continues: "The apostle Paul states in the eleventh chapter of Romans that the fall of the Jews was a blessing to the rest of the world. He speaks of it as the enriching of the Gentiles and the reconciling of the world. The catastrophe of Jerusalem really signalized the beginning of a new and world-wide Kingdom, marking the full separation of the Christian Church from legalistic Judaism. The whole system of worship, so closely associated with Jerusalem and the Temple, received, as it were, a death blow from God himself. God was now through with the Old Covenant made at Sinai: holding full sway was the sign of the New Covenant."[39]

The early Christians who first read the Book of Revelation, especially those of a Jewish background, had to understand that the destruction of Jerusalem would not mean the end of Covenant or Kingdom. The fall of old Israel was not "the beginning of the end." Instead, it was the sign that Christ's worldwide Kingdom had truly begun, that their Lord was ruling the nations from His heavenly throne, and that the eventual conquest of all nations by the armies of Christ was assured. For these humble, suffering Believers, the promised age of the Messiah's rule had arrived. And what they were about to witness in the fall of Israel was the end of the Beginning.

Jonathan Welton in his book Raptureless explains the Revelation this way:

> [40]Reading the Book of Revelation can be very confusing because it is filled with symbols that require interpretation, and it is also filled with repetition. The seals, the trumpets, the seven figures, and the bowls all depict the same events of the AD 70 destruction in different ways and from different angles. They are not exact parallels, but each repeating scene emphasizes something new. Some might wonder, why would this be with repeating patterns? What does this represent?

Apostle John's prophecy is related to the message of Leviticus 26. Like Deuteronomy 28, Leviticus 26 sets forth the sanctions of the [Mosaic] Covenant: If Israel obeys God, she will be blessed in every area of life

---

[39] Ibid., p. 138.
[40] Welton, Jonathan. Raptureless: An Optimistic Guide to the End of the World - Revised Edition Including The Art of Revelation. BookBaby. Kindle Edition.

(Leviticus 26:1–13; Deuteronomy 28:1–14); if she disobeys, however, she will be visited with the curse, spelled out in horrifying detail (Leviticus 26:14–39; Deuteronomy 28:15–68). (These curses were most fully poured out in the progressive desolation of Israel during the "Last Days", culminating in the Great Tribulation of A.D. 67–70, as punishment for her apostasy and rejection of her True Husband, the Lord Jesus Christ.).

TRUMPET 1: REVELATION 8:6-7 HAIL AND FIRE RAIN DOWN

Now the seven angels who had the seven trumpets made ready to blow them. The first angel blew his trumpet, and there followed hail and fire, mixed with blood, which fell on the earth; and a third of the earth was burnt up, and a third of the trees were burnt up, and all green grass was burnt up.

After the first trumpet, hail and fire rain down upon the local land of Israel (ge).

TRUMPET 2: REVELATION 8:8-9 A MOUNTAIN THROWN INTO THE SEA

The second angel blew his trumpet, and something like a great mountain, burning with fire, was thrown into the sea; and a third of the sea became blood, a third of the living creatures in the sea died, and a third of the ships were destroyed.

The symbol of the second trumpet has been distorted by many over the last two thousand years. The most popular theory recently projects an asteroid will crash into the ocean and kill a third of the sea creatures and destroy a third of all ships. In reality, if an asteroid that big is going to crash into the earth, the Book of Revelation should end right there; such an asteroid would literally move earth off its axis, and all life on earth would immediately either burn up or freeze because of the planet moving closer to or away from the sun. Clearly, we are dealing with a symbol. So, we must ask ourselves, what would the mountain represent to John's readers? The most obvious answer is that the First Century Jewish Believers would have interpreted this mountain in Revelation as a symbol of Jerusalem, God's holy mountain (see Exodus 15:17).

Again, Chilton gives stunning insight:

> Connect this [Revelation 8:8] with the fact that Jesus, in the middle of a lengthy series of discourses and parables about the destruction of Jerusalem (Matt. 20-25), cursed an unfruitful fig tree, as a symbol of judgment upon Israel. He then told His disciples, "Truly I say to you, if you have faith, and do not doubt, you shall say to this mountain, 'Be taken up and cast into the sea,' it shall happen. And all things you ask in prayer, believing, you shall receive' (Matthew 21:21-22). Was Jesus being flippant? Did He really expect His disciples to go around praying about moving literal mountains? Of course not. More importantly, Jesus was not changing the subject. He was still giving them a lesson about the fall of Israel. What was the lesson? Jesus was instructing His disciples to pray imprecatory prayers, beseeching God to destroy Israel, to wither the fig tree, to cast the apostate mountain into the sea.
>
> And that is exactly what happened. The persecuted Church, under the oppression from the apostate Jews, began praying for God's vengeance upon Israel (Revelation 6:9-11), calling for the mountain of Israel to *"be taken up and cast into the sea."*
> Their offerings were received at God's heavenly altar, and in response God directed His angels to throw down His judgments to the Land (Revelation 8:3-5).[41]
> Thus, in amazing simplicity, the mountain falling into the sea is a symbol of Jerusalem's destruction.

TRUMPET 3: REVELATION 8:10-11 A STAR FALLING

The third angel blew his trumpet, and a great star fell from heaven, blazing like a torch, and it fell on a third of the rivers and on the fountains of water. The name of the star is Wormwood. A third of the waters became wormwood, and many men died of the water, because it was made bitter.

---

[41] *Ibid.*, 238-239.

The First Century Jewish reader would have grasped this key to understanding the third trumpet: The star is named Wormwood and turned a third of the water into wormwood. Modern readers seem to gloss over the mention of wormwood and focus entirely on the falling star. As I mentioned before, Revelation has four repetitions within its judgments. This star connects to the sixth seal and the stars that fell to the earth (see Revelation 6:13). But even more important to understanding this passage is the definition of wormwood.

Wormwood is a specific term used in the Old Testament to warn Israel of its destruction as a punishment for apostasy. The following passages demonstrate this clearly: Deuteronomy 29:18 NKJV

So that there may not be among you man or woman or family or tribe, whose heart turns away today from the LORD our God, to go and serve the gods of these nations, and that there may not be among you a root bearing bitterness or wormwood.

Therefore, thus says the LORD of hosts, the God of Israel: "Behold, I will feed them, this people, with wormwood, and give them water of gall to drink" (Jeremiah 9:15 NKJV).

Therefore, thus says the LORD of hosts concerning the prophets: "Behold, I will feed them with wormwood, and make them drink the water of gall; for from the prophets of Jerusalem profaneness has gone out into all the land" (Jeremiah 23:15 NKJV).

He has filled me with bitterness, He has made me drink wormwood.... Remember my affliction and roaming, the wormwood and the gall (Lamentations 3:15, 19 NKJV).

You who turn justice to wormwood, and lay righteousness to rest in the earth (Amos 5:7 NKJV).

Thus, we can see that, when John mentioned Wormwood, the original readers would have understood he was declaring the apostasy of Jerusalem.

TRUMPET 4: REVELATION 8:12-13 CELESTIAL BODIES DISTURBED

> *The fourth angel blew his trumpet, and a third of the sun was struck, and a third of the moon, and a third of the stars, so that a third of their light was darkened; a third of the day was kept from shining, and likewise a third of the night. Then I looked, and I heard an eagle crying with a loud voice, as it flew in midheaven, "Woe, woe, woe to those who dwell on the earth, at the blasts of the other trumpets which the three angels are about to blow!"*

The fourth trumpet is another obvious parallel to the sixth seal (see Revelation 6:12–14), which uses the same prophetic language explained in [42]Raptureless regarding Matthew 24:29. In short, celestial disturbances are used as a prophetic idiom throughout Scripture to point to the destruction of a city.

TRUMPET 5: REVELATION 9:1-6 LOCUSTS FROM THE PIT

> *And the fifth angel blew his trumpet, and I saw a star fallen from heaven to earth, and he was given the key of the shaft of the bottomless pit; he opened the shaft of the bottomless pit, and from the shaft rose smoke like the smoke of a great furnace, and the sun and the air were darkened with the smoke from the shaft. Then from the smoke came locusts on the earth, and they were given power like the power of scorpions of the earth; they were told not to harm the grass of the earth or any green growth or any tree, but only those of mankind who have not the seal of God upon their foreheads; they were allowed to torture them for five months, but not to kill them, and their torture was like the torture of a scorpion, when it stings a man. And in those days men will seek death and will not find it; they will long to die, and death will fly from them.*

---

[42] Welton, Jonathan. Raptureless: An Optimistic Guide to the End of the World

Let's go back for a moment to our illustration of the painting. As an author, it seems to me like the fifth trumpet of Revelation is like a dark and foreboding corner of the painting that is not well understood and is so dark and mysterious that one cannot help but stand and stare in wonder. I will attempt to give what I find to be a reasonable explanation—essentially John was depicting the demonic state into which Jerusalem had devolved before the Roman destruction. Yet I know this will not answer every question for every reader.

But as James Stuart Russell wrote, "With our attention fixed on a single spot of earth, and absolutely shut up to a very brief space of time, it is comparatively easy to read the symbols, and still more satisfactory to mark their perfect correspondence with facts."[43]

When we keep in mind that these symbols are about the 70 AD destruction of Jerusalem, it becomes easier for us to find the proper interpretation.

I will start with a quote from Victorious Eschatology that I found most helpful:

> Some of the most well-known futurist teachers say that these locusts from the bottomless pit are futuristic helicopters that swarm out of the sky and shoot out of their tails a poison that inflicts great pain. Other noted futurists have observed the recent uprising of Islamic terrorists and concluded that the locusts must be the Muslim extremists who will someday attack God's people. These interpretations of the futurists are interesting because these are the same futurist teachers that claim to be taking the Bible literally. If we take those verses literally then we have to believe that actual locusts with gold crowns, faces like men, hair like women, teeth like lions, and tails like scorpions will swarm across the earth.
>
> Furthermore, if the futurist teachers were taking the Scriptures literally, they would have to say that their helicopters or their Muslim terrorists were coming out of a bottomless pit. Of course, no futurist could reasonably say that. The idea that futurist Christians take the book of Revelation literally is a myth.[44]

---

[43] James Stuart Russell, *The Parousia*, 411.
[44] *Victorious Eschatology*, Eberle and Trench, 155.

[It is also interesting to note that the time period mentioned with in fifth trumpet (five months) corresponds with the actual seasonal length of the locusts in that region (May–September)]. We must consider what the First Century Jew would have understood when they heard the description in John's vision.

First, they would have connected the locusts to the eighth plague upon Egypt (see Exodus 10).

Second, they would note the plague would be upon the non-Christians, whereas the Christians were "marked" and protected just as Israel was during the Egyptian plagues. Essentially this picture showed them that Jerusalem had become Egypt in the eyes of Heaven and that the Christians were enacting a new exodus. We should note here that Revelation 11:8 makes it very clear that Jerusalem, *"the city in which our Lord was killed,"* had become *"Sodom and Egypt."* Even here in the fifth trumpet, we find the eighth plague upon Egypt, but we also find language that mirrors the destruction of Sodom.

When he opened the Abyss, smoke rose from it like the smoke from a gigantic furnace (Revelation 9:2a NKJV).

He looked down toward Sodom and Gomorrah, toward all the land of the plain, and he saw dense smoke rising from the land, like smoke from a furnace (Genesis 19:28 NKJV).

One other perspective on the fifth trumpet is that it represented the total demonization of Jerusalem before the destruction by Rome. In fact, Josephus wrote of how evil Jerusalem had become, saying that if Rome hadn't come to destroy them, the earth might have simply opened and swallowed them. This is a very revealing quote from a Jewish non-Christian observer:

"I am of opinion" he says "that had the Romans deferred the punishment of these wretches, either the earth would have opened, and swallowed up the city, or it would have been swept away by a deluge or have shared in the thunderbolts of the land of Sodom. For it produced a race far more ungodly than those who were thus visited [i.e., more evil than Sodom].[45]

---

[45] James Stuart Russell, *The Parousia*, 412.

How could Jerusalem have been truly that evil? Though it may be hard for us to believe, Jesus did declare they would be that evil in Matthew 12:

Matthew 12:41–45 NKJV
The men of Nineveh will stand up at the judgment with this generation and condemn it; for they repented at the preaching of Jonah, and now something greater than Jonah is here. The Queen of the South will rise at the judgment with this generation and condemn it; for she came from the ends of the earth to listen to Solomon's wisdom, and now something greater than Solomon is here. When an impure spirit comes out of a person, it goes through arid places seeking rest and does not find it. Then it says, "I will return to the house I left." When it arrives, it finds the house unoccupied, swept clean and put in order. Then it goes and takes with it seven other spirits more wicked than itself, and they go in and live there. And the final condition of that person is worse than the first. That is how it will be with this wicked generation.

Jesus was not giving a teaching on deliverance or healing. He was declaring that even though His ministry was cleaning up Jerusalem spiritually, once He was done, the people would quickly refill Jerusalem with evil, even seven times worse! And that is exactly what happened historically, which is why Josephus gave such a harsh evaluation of Jerusalem.

Thus, the locusts from the pit represent the utter demonization of Jerusalem in preparation for their destruction.

TRUMPET 6: REVELATION 9:13-16 FOUR ANGELS AND 200 MILLION?

Then the sixth angel blew his trumpet, and I heard a voice from the four horns of the golden altar before God, saying to the sixth angel who had the trumpet, "Release the four angels who are bound at the great river Euphra'tes." So the four angels were released, who had been held ready for the hour, the day, the month, and the year, to kill a third of mankind. The number of the troops of cavalry was twice ten thousand times ten thousand; I heard their number.

History records that Titus had four military legions stationed at the Euphrates that advanced upon and destroyed Jerusalem. This is pictured in John's vision of four mighty angels who are unleashed to kill and bring destruction.

This trumpet also includes the mysterious number, *"Twice ten thousand times ten thousand."* Many fanciful explanations have been created regarding this number. Some translators have even simply multiplied it and say the army is 200 million. Yet in this passage, we are dealing with prophetic idioms that are two thousand years old, and we must ask, what would twice ten thousand times ten thousand have meant to the original readers?

In the Old Testament, ten thousand was used to represent an overwhelming and nearly impossible foe. For example, *"Saul has slain his thousands, and David his tens of thousands"* (1 Samuel 18:7, 21:11). So, in this passage, we find John declaring ten thousand times ten thousand and twice over! Basically, he was saying, "Jerusalem, there is no deliverance for you; you are absolutely and unquestionably doomed!"

We must keep in mind that Revelation is a book full of symbols.

First, in Revelation 11:8, John gives us a huge key to interpreting Revelation when he clearly refers to the "great city" as the city where our *"Lord was crucified."* In other words, he tells us plainly that it is First Century Jerusalem, which is figuratively called Sodom and Egypt. Thus, when we read in Revelation 17 that the whore of Babylon is the great city, we know the whore was Jerusalem, and when we read that Babylon, the great city has fallen, we know it speaks of the destruction of Jerusalem. In this way, Revelation 11:8 is a major key to understanding the theme of Revelation—the judgment of First Century Jerusalem and the establishment of the heavenly Jerusalem. Every time we read "the great city," it is a clear reference to Jerusalem: Revelation 16:19 NKJV

> *The great city split into three parts, and the cities of the nations collapsed. God remembered Babylon the Great and gave her the cup filled with the wine of the fury of his wrath.*
>
> *The woman you saw is the great city that rules over the kings of the earth* (Revelation 17:18 NKJV).

Terrified at her torment, they will stand far off and cry: "Woe! Woe to you, great city, you mighty city of Babylon! In one hour, your doom has come!"...and cry out: "Woe! Woe to you, great city, dressed in fine linen, purple and scarlet, and glittering with gold, precious stones and pearls!".... When they see the smoke of her burning, they will exclaim, "Was there ever a city like this great city?" They will throw dust on their heads, and with weeping and mourning cry out: "Woe! Woe to you, great city, where all who had ships on the sea became rich through her wealth! In one hour, she has been brought to ruin!"... Then a mighty angel picked up a boulder the size of a large millstone and threw it into the sea and said: "With such violence the great city of Babylon will be thrown down, never to be found again" (Revelation 18:10, 16, 18–19, 21 NKJV).

Now let's look back at verse 7, where the two witnesses are killed. The question is, *If the two witnesses represent the Law and the Prophets, how can they be put to death?* I believe the two witnesses (the Old Testament Law and Prophets) were witnessing about Jesus to the Jews before the AD 70 destruction, but ultimately the Law and the Prophets were ignored, rejected, and "killed" by the Jews.

The Law and the Prophets testified as witnesses of Jesus as the Messiah-King and of Israel as the covenant-breaking nation that stood guilty. Even Jesus, during His life on earth, referred to the Old Testament as a witness of Him: John 5:39 NKJV

You study the Scriptures diligently because you think that in them you have eternal life. These are the very Scriptures that testify about me.

I agree with Eberle and Trench's explanation of the two witnesses:

The Law and the Prophets were witnesses against the Jewish people. The Jews had been unfaithful in their covenant with God, and therefore, judgment was coming upon them. However, the Law and the Prophets were also the authoritative witnesses of the early Church. As Christians witnessed to the Jews about Jesus Christ, they did not have a New Testament from which to preach. They spoke from the Law and the Prophets, convincing many that

Jesus was the Christ. Again, we see how the Law and the Prophets were sounding throughout the streets of Jerusalem.[46]

This idea is even more fully exemplified in the next two verses: Revelation 11:9–10 NKJV

For three and a half days some from every people, tribe, language and nation will gaze on their bodies and refuse them burial. The inhabitants of the earth will gloat over them and will celebrate by sending each other gifts, because these two Prophets had tormented those who live on the earth.

In other words, the AD 70 world was happy to see Jerusalem destroyed and, with it, all the Old Testament rules, regulations, sacrifices, and ceremonies. As Eberle and Trench put it:

In what way were the Law and the Prophets put to death? When Jerusalem was destroyed by the Roman army, it appeared that everything in which the Jews had put their trust had failed. All had ended. How could they ever rise again? It seemed impossible. While the two witnesses were silent, the people throughout the Gentile world rejoiced because the Law and the Prophets also bore witness against them and their sins. After the dust from Jerusalem's destruction had settled, "the breath of life from God" came back into the two witnesses (Revelation 11:10). The voice of the Law and the Prophets rose again. Then the two witnesses were called back into heaven (Revelation 11:12), but at that same time "there was a great earthquake" (Revelation 11:13). As we have discussed before, in apocalyptic language earthquakes represented a demolition or transfer of authority. Indeed, two witnesses were taken to heaven, but the Law and the Prophets continued to sound through the Church. The voices of two witnesses were transferred to the Church, and hence, the Law and the Prophets continue sounding forth the voice of God even today.[47]

Thus, the testifying, death, and resurrection of the two witnesses symbolize the transition between the Old and New Covenants. Here is the culmination: Revelation 11:11–12 NKJV

---

[46] Victorious Eschatology, Eberle and Trench, 163.
[47] *Ibid.,* 163-164.

But after the three and a half days the breath of life from God entered them, and they stood on their feet, and terror struck those who saw them. Then they heard a loud voice from Heaven saying to them, "Come up here." And they went up to heaven in a cloud, while their enemies looked on.

The Kingdom of Jesus revived the Old Testament witness, and instead of a religion full of rules in the earthly Jerusalem, Jesus formed Christianity on the foundation of the Old Covenant, enabling His followers to partake of the heavenly Jerusalem.

TRUMPET 7: REVELATION: 11:15-19 JESUS WINS

Then the seventh angel blew his trumpet, and there were loud voices in heaven, saying, "The kingdom of the world has become the kingdom of our Lord and of his Christ, and he shall reign for ever and ever." And the twenty-four elders who sit on their thrones before God fell on their faces and worshiped God, saying, "We give thanks to thee, Lord God Almighty, who art and who wast, that thou hast taken thy great power and begun to reign. The nations raged, but thy wrath came, and the time for the dead to be judged, for rewarding thy servants, the prophets and saints, and those who fear thy name, both small and great, and for destroying the destroyers of the earth." Then God's temple in heaven was opened, and the ark of his covenant was seen within his temple; and there were flashes of lightning, voices, peals of thunder, an earthquake, and heavy hail.

At the seventh trumpet, Jesus is declared the victor, and the Ark of the Covenant is shown to permanently reside in Heaven.

The original Ark of the Old Covenant had gone missing hundreds of years earlier. Now, John watched this vision, he saw an Ark in Heaven! This is not that old Ark; it is the Ark of the New Covenant. The New Covenant is between the Father and the Son; therefore, the Ark that contains the New Covenant resides in Heaven.[48]

In the next chapter we would like to have a look at the two conflicting realities: The mark of the beast and The Seal of God.

---

[48] End of section from Welton, Jonathan. Raptureless: An Optimistic Guide to the End of the World - Revised Edition Including The Art of Revelation. BookBaby. Kindle Edition.

CHAPTER SEVEN
THE MARK OF THE BEAST AND THE SEAL OF GOD

As we continue, I ask you to remember that we are studying the Revelation with the understanding that it was written prior to the AD 70 destruction of the Temple, and that most of this prophecy has been fulfilled during the First Century and the fall of the Temple.

Also, as we continue our study of the prophecy let us now look at two conflicting realities, from Revelation 12:1 – 15:4.

Here we witness the war of the Church of Jesus Christ against Her enemies and her victory. And this ends with the Church becoming God's New Holy Temple replacing the Old Covenant Temple! And I do believe that this war is ongoing. And even though we know that Jesus has already defeated the devil, we need to be able to enforce that victory by our lifestyle through every generation.

Milton S. Terry in his book reveals the following with which I wholeheartedly agree:

> "This reveals the Church in conflict with infernal and worldly principalities and powers, surviving all persecution, and triumphing by the word of her testimony, and, after Babylon the harlot falls and passes from view, appearing as the wife of the Lamb, the tabernacle of God with men, glorious in her beauty and imperishable as the throne of God."[49]

---
[49] Milton S. Terry, *Biblical Apocalyptics: A Study of the Most Notable Revelations of God and of Christ in the Canonical Scriptures* (New York: Eaton & Mains, 1896), p. 381.

We see this conflict being recorded in the first few verses of Revelation 12:1-6

And a great portent appeared in heaven, a woman clothed with the sun, with the moon under her feet, and on her head a crown of twelve stars; she was with child and she cried out in her pangs of birth, in anguish for delivery. And another portent appeared in heaven; behold, a great red dragon, with seven heads and ten horns, and seven diadems upon his heads. His tail swept down a third of the stars of heaven, and cast them to the earth. And the dragon stood before the woman who was about to bear a child, that he might devour her child when she brought it forth; she brought forth a male child, one who is to rule all the nations with a rod of iron, but her child was caught up to God and to his throne, and the woman fled into the wilderness, where she has a place prepared by God, in which to be nourished for one thousand two hundred and sixty days

Here in Revelation 12 we see a glorious vision of the Church in her purity, as the wife of God: She is, in the image of her Husband (Ps. 104:2; Revelation 1:16; 10:1), clothed with the sun (cf. Isaiah 60:1-2). The moon under her feet and her crown of twelve stars enhance the picture of glory and dominion – indeed, of her ascent from glory to glory (I Corinthians 15:41; 2 Corinthians 3:18).

The dragon's goal here was to abort the work of Jesus Christ. To devour and kill Him. *So,* **the dragon stood** (cf. *Genesis 3:14)* **before the woman** *in order to* **devour her Child,** *to kill Jesus Christ as soon as He was born.*

This conflict between Christ and satan was announced in Genesis 3:15, the war between the two seeds, the Seed of the Woman and the seed of the serpent. From the first book of the Bible to the last, this is the basic warfare of history. The dragon is at war with the Woman and her Seed, primarily Jesus Christ. All throughout history satan was trying either to keep Christ from being born, or to kill Him as soon as He was born.

This is why Cain killed Abel, under the inspiration of the dragon: The attack on Abel was an attempt to destroy the Seed. It was unsuccessful, for Eve then gave birth to Seth, the Appointed One, "in place of Abel" (Genesis 4:25 – *And Adam knew his wife again,* **and she bore a son and named** him Seth, *"For God has appointed another seed for me instead of Abel, whom Cain killed."*), and the Seed was preserved in him. satan's next tactic was to corrupt the line of Seth; thus, within ten generations from Adam, virtually all Seth's descendants apostatized through intermarriage with the heathen (Genesis 6:1-12), and the whole earth was corrupted except for one righteous man and his family. satan's mad rage to attack the Seed was so great that the entire world was destroyed, yet still he failed. The Seed was preserved within a single family in the Ark. *Are you seeing this? Our God is a Master Genius, yes, He is!*

The dragon again tried to murder the Seed in his attacks on the family of Abraham. This pattern came to a dramatic climax at the birth of Jesus Christ, when the dragon possesses King Herod, the Edomite ruler of Judea, and inspires him to slaughter the children of Bethlehem (Matthew 2:13-18); indeed, John's vision of the Woman, the Child, and the dragon seems almost an allegory of that event. The dragon tried again, of course: tempting the Lord (Luke 4:1-13), seeking to have Him murdered (Luke 4:28-29), subjecting Him to human and demonic oppression throughout His ministry, possessing one of the most trusted disciples to betray Him (John 13:2, 27), and finally orchestrating His crucifixion.

The most striking example of this pattern on a large scale occurs throughout the history of Israel, from the Exodus to the Exile: The Covenant people's perennial, consistent temptation to murder their own children, to offer them up as sacrifices to demons (Leviticus 18:21; 2 Kings 16:3; 2 Chronicles 28:3; Psalms 106:37-38; Ezekiel 16:20). Why? It was the war of the two seeds. The dragon was trying to destroy the Christ. The dragon was finally and permanently defeated, at the Cross. The Cross was God's way of tricking satan into fulfilling His purposes, according to His wisdom – *"the hidden wisdom,"* Apostle Paul says, *"which God predestined before the ages to our glory, the wisdom which none of the rulers of this age has understood; for if they had understood it, they would not have crucified the Lord of glory"* (1 Corinthians 2:7-8). In wounding the Seed's heel, the serpent's head was crushed, as was prophesied at the beginning in Genesis 3:15 *"I will put enmity between you and the woman, and between your seed and her seed; he shall bruise your head, and you shall bruise his heel."*

Chapter 12 then goes on to describe the war from the heavenly aspect, with Michael the Archangel waging a war against the dragon and defeating it. Here is what is shown: Revelation 12:7-12

> *Now war arose in heaven, Michael and his angels fighting against the dragon; and the dragon and his angels fought, but they were defeated and there was no longer any place for them in heaven. And the great dragon was thrown down, that ancient serpent, who is called the devil and satan, the deceiver of the whole world—he was thrown down to the earth, and his angels were thrown down with him. And I heard a loud voice in heaven, saying, "Now the salvation and the power and the kingdom of our God and the authority of his Christ have come, for the accuser of our brethren has been thrown down, who accuses them day and night before our God. And they have conquered him by the blood of the Lamb and by the word of their testimony, for they loved not their lives even unto death. Rejoice then, O heaven and you that dwell therein! But woe to you, O earth and sea, for the devil has come down to you in great wrath, because he knows that his time is short!".*

We have already noted that the Holy War was initiated by the attack of Michael and the army of Heaven. In response, the dragon and his angels waged war. But this defensive action by the forces of evil proved an utter failure: They were not strong enough, and there was no longer a place found for them in Heaven. And the great dragon was thrown down, in abject defeat. For the forces of evil, the battle is lost. This is exactly what Jesus prophesied about the prospects for His Church Militant: *"And I also say to you that you are Peter, and on this rock I will build My church, and the gates of Hades shall not prevail against it."* (Matthew 16:18).

John interjects detailed information about the dragon's identity: He is the serpent of old, the ancient tempter who seduced Eve in the beginning (Genesis 3:1-15). The dragon is known as the devil, a term meaning *the slanderer,* for he is, as the Lord said, *"a liar, and the father of the lie"* (John 8:44). A related term for the dragon is satan (or, more properly, *the satan),* the Hebrew word for an adversary, especially in legal matters. The being whom we call *satan* is the attorney for the prosecution, the accuser who brings up legal charges against men in God's court, the evil one who tirelessly accuses the brethren "day and night" (Revelation 12:10). satan was the accuser of Job (Job 1:6-11; 2:1-5) and of Joshua the high priest (Zechariah 3:1-10)-and, as can be seen from both of those cases, his supposedly legal accusations are mere lies. The accuser of God's people is a slanderer, the Father of the lie. Because he is the liar *par excellence,* he deceives the whole world. It was satan who was behind the slanderous accusations against the early Christians, the scurrilous rumors and criminal charges alleging that they were apostates, atheists, ritual murderers, cannibals, social revolutionaries, and haters of mankind.[50]

This great apocalyptic battle, the greatest fight in all history, has already been fought and won by the Lord Jesus Christ, John says, and the dragon has been overthrown. Moreover, the martyrs who spent their lives in Christ's service did not die in vain; they are partakers in the victory: *"They conquered the dragon by the blood of the Lamb"* (Revelation 12:11)

The Holy War between Michael and the dragon therefore cannot possibly be a portrayal of the final battle of history at the end of the world. It cannot be future at all. The question then that needs to be asked and answered is this:

When was satan completely cut off from Heaven? He definitively fell, during the ministry of Christ, culminating in the atonement, the resurrection, and the ascension of the Lord to His heavenly throne. As we read through the accounts of Jesus' life on earth, we could see the different stages of the Holy War throughout the message of the Gospels. Whereas the activity of demons seems relatively rare in the Old Testament, in the New Testament, it records numerous outbreaks of demonism. As one opens the pages of the New Testament, demons are almost inescapable. Why? What made the difference? I believe that it was the Presence of Jesus Christ. When He came on the scene He went on the offensive, entering history to do battle with the dragon, and immediately the dragon sought to counterattack, fighting back with all his might, wreaking as much havoc as possible. And when we see the Lord warring against the devil, we also see Him being given angelic assistance (cf. Matthew 4:11; 26:53; Luke 22:43). In like manner as Michael leading the Angels, Jesus Christ led His Apostles against the dragon, driving him out of his position. The message of the Gospels is that in the earthly ministry of Jesus Christ and His disciples, satan lost his place of power and fell down to the earth. See Luke 10:17-20

> *The seventy returned with joy, saying, "Lord, even the demons are subject to us in your name!" And he said to them, "I saw satan fall*

---

[50] Cf. Robert L. Wilken, *The Christians as the Romans Saw Them* (New Haven: Yale University Press, 1984).

like lightning from heaven. Behold, I have given you authority to tread upon serpents and scorpions, and over all the power of the enemy; and nothing shall hurt you. Nevertheless do not rejoice in this, that the spirits are subject to you; but rejoice that your names are written in heaven."

The message of Revelation is consistent with that of the New Testament as a whole: Christ has arrived, satan has been thrown down, and the Kingdom has come. By His death and resurrection, Christ "disarmed" the demons, triumphing over them (Colossians 2:15). satan has been rendered powerless (Hebrews 2:14-15), and so St. Paul was able to assure the Believers in Rome that "the God of peace will soon crush satan under your feet" (Romans 16:20). The Cross was the mark, Jesus said, of the judgment of the world.[51] (John 12:31) or, as John Calvin rendered it, the reformation and restoration of the world. The illegitimate ruler of the world was cast out by the coming of Christ. As He announced at His Ascension, *"All authority (exousia) in heaven and on earth has been given to Me"* (Matthew 28:18). Apostle John's vision declares the same thing: The Kingdom of our God and the authority *(exousia)* of His Christ have come!

However, Christ's definitive conquest of the dragon does not mean the end of his activity altogether. Indeed, like a cornered rat he becomes even more frantically vicious, his snarling rage increasing with his frustration and impotence. The Voice from Heaven thus declares: *Woe to* **the Land** *and the Sea, because the dragon has come down to you, having great wrath, knowing that he has only a short time.* (Revelation 12:12).

It is important for our interpretation to note also that the persecution of the Woman arises in connection with the dragon's fall to **the Land** [the Land here being referred to is that of Israel]. It is there, first of all, that he seeks to destroy the Church. The young Church that was just beginning to arise in the earth. The first set of membership was that of the Jewish Saints.

Now, please understand this: The Book of Revelation is a Covenant document. It is a prophecy, like the prophecies of the Old Testament. This means that it is not concerned with making "predictions" of astonishing

---

[51] John Calvin, *Commentary on the Gospel According to John* (Grand Rapids: Baker Book House, 1979), Vol. 2, p. 36; cf. Ronald S. Wallace, *Calvin's Doctrine of the Christian Life* (Tyler, TX: Geneva Ministries, [1959] 1982), p. 110.

events as such. As prophecy, its focus is redemptive and ethical. Its concern is with the Covenant. The Bible is God's revelation about His Covenant with His people. It was written to show what God has done to save His people and glorify Himself through them.

Therefore, when God speaks of the Roman Empire in the Book of Revelation, His purpose is not to tell us titillating bits of gossip about life at Nero's court. He speaks of Rome only in relation to the Covenant and the history of redemption. "We should keep in mind that in all this prophetic symbolism we have before us *the Roman empire as a persecuting power.* This Apocalypse is not concerned with the history of Rome. The beast is not a symbol of Rome, but of the great *Roman world-power,* conceived as the organ of the old serpent, the devil, and satan to persecute the scattered Saints of God."· The most important fact about Rome, from the viewpoint of Revelation, is not that it is a powerful state, but that it is *the beast,* in opposition to the God of the Covenant; the issue is not essentially political but religious. The Roman Empire is not seen in terms of itself, but solely in terms of 1) *the Land* (Israel), and 2) *the Church.*

Then, in chapter 13 we are introduced to the two beasts, the beast of the sea and the beast of the earth. Nothing in Revelation has been subject to as much speculation and misinformation as the beast from the sea. This has been the source of the modern paranoia regarding implanted microchips and barcodes. The type of interpretation that takes place regarding the mysterious number 666, is nothing short of being ridiculous and just mere fantasy.

[52]THE BEAST OF THE SEA

What would John's original readers have understood this beast to be? With absolute certainty, I say they would have seen the beast from the sea as Nero and the Roman Empire. The apostle John refers to the number 666 and says in verse 18, *"This calls for wisdom. Let the person who has insight calculate the number of the beast, for it is the number of a man. That number is 666."* When we read this verse, we must keep the following details in mind:

1. John was expecting his readers to be able to calculate this number and all arrive at the same conclusion.

---
[52] Welton, Jonathan. Raptureless: An Optimistic Guide to the End of the World - Revised Edition Including The Art of Revelation. BookBaby. Kindle Edition.

2. John was not writing to readers thousands of years in the future but to his immediate contemporaries, and he expected them to arrive at the right interpretation.
3. John was not referring to a deep, profound mystery but to natural knowledge when he said, *"this calls for wisdom" and "insight [to] calculate."* He said this because the number code he used was the ancient Hebrew and not the concurrent Greek language of the day. **Again, remember he was primarily speaking to Jewish Christians who knew the Old Covenant, as we did not as yet have the New Testament Scriptures!**
4. When the Jewish readers saw what John wrote, they would have mentally translated the numeric value into its corresponding Hebrew letters and spelled out Nrwn Qsr, or as we would pronounce it, Nero Caesar.
5. Some variants of the text say the number is 616 [check the margin of your Bible], which simply spells out Nero's name in a secondary manner, further solidifying this interpretation. (For more on that, see Kenneth Gentry's book, The Book of Revelation Made Easy).

THE BEAST OF THE EARTH

The beast from the earth is more accurately translated as the beast from the land (ge), which is the land of Israel. Nero was called the beast that arose from the sea because, if one was standing on the shore near Jerusalem looking out to sea, Rome was the major city directly across the sea. By contrast, this beast arose from within the land of Israel. To the early Church reading John's vision, the beast that had arisen in the local region of Jerusalem was the Temple rulers, the priestly aristocracy that operated under the power and in the presence of the sea beast as a delegated authority (see Revelation 13:12). After describing these two beasts, in Revelation 14, the scene changes again, and John sees Jesus (as the Lamb) standing with the Christians (the 144,000) who escaped the destruction by fleeing to the safety of Mount Pella. At the same time, below the mountain the three angels fly over Jerusalem (Babylon) declaring her destruction below. [End of quote.[53]]

Just as the beast from the sea was in the image of the dragon, so we see another creature who is in the Image of the beast. Apostle John saw

---
[53] *Ibid.*

this one **coming up from the Land,** arising from within Israel itself. In 16:13 and 19:20, we are told the identity of this **land beast**. He is the **false prophet**, representing what Jesus had foretold would take place in Israel's last days: Matthew 24:5, 11

> *For many will come in my name, saying, 'I am the Christ,' and they will lead many astray. ... And many false prophets will arise and lead many astray.*

The rise of the false prophets paralleled that of the antichrists; but whereas the antichrists had apostatized into Judaism from within the Church, the false prophets were Jewish religious leaders who sought to seduce Christians from the outside. As Cornelis Vanderwaal has noted, "In Scripture, false prophecy appears only within the covenant context";[54] it is the imitation of true prophecy and operates in relation to the Covenant people. Moses had warned that false prophets would arise *from among* the Covenant people, performing signs and wonders (Deuteronomy 13:1-5).

THE MESSAGE FROM THE THREE ANGELS: REVELATION 14:6-11

> *Then I saw another angel flying in midheaven, with an eternal gospel to proclaim to those who dwell on earth, to every nation and tribe and tongue and people; and he said with a loud voice, "Fear God and give him glory, for the hour of his judgment has come; and worship him who made heaven and earth, the sea and the fountains of water." Another angel, a second, followed, saying, "Fallen, fallen is Babylon the great, she who made all nations drink the wine of her impure passion." And another angel, a third, followed them, saying with a loud voice, "If any one worships the beast and its image, and receives a mark on his forehead or on his hand, he also shall drink the wine of God's wrath, poured unmixed into the cup of his anger, and he shall be tormented with fire and sulphur in the presence of the holy angels and in the presence of the Lamb. And the smoke of their torment goes up for ever and ever; and they have no rest, day or night, these worshipers of the beast and its image, and whoever receives the mark of its name."*

---

[54] Cornelis Vanderwaal, *Search the Scriptures,* Vol. 10: *Hebrews-Revelation* (St. Catherines, Ontario: Paideia Press, 1979), p. 89; cf. p. 100.

First, Apostle John sees another angel flying in mid-heaven, the sphere of the Eagle's cries of woe to the Land (8:13). But this angel preaches peace: The coming judgment is not an end in itself, but part of the proclamation of the eternal Gospel. Contrary to the speculations of several expositors, there is no reason to suppose that this is something other than the Gospel of which the New Testament constantly speaks. It is the message of the coming of the Kingdom, as John and Jesus Christ had announced from the beginning: *"In those days came John the Baptist, preaching in the wilderness of Judea, "Repent, for the kingdom of heaven is at hand." (Matthew 3:1-2); "Now after John was arrested, Jesus came into Galilee, preaching the gospel of God, and saying, "The time is fulfilled, and the kingdom of God is at hand; repent, and believe in the gospel."* (Mark 1:14-15).

And this is the Gospel preached by the angel, every element in it an aspect of the New Testament message: The angel preaches this Gospel to those who sit over the Land. The usual expression for the Israelite apostates is *those who dwell in the Land* (3:10; 13:8, 12, 14; 17:2, 8). This time, attention is focused on the message to the authorities of Israel, those who are seated or enthroned over the Land (the verb is the same as that used in verse 14 of the Son of Man enthroned on the Cloud). The Gospel message commanded the rulers of Palestine to submit to the lordship of Jesus Christ, to honor Him, rather than Caesar, as God. But the rulers and authorities rejected Him, saying *"We will not have this Man to rule over us!"* (Luke 19:14).

The Lord Himself proclaimed the glory and judgment of God to the authorities of Israel (Matthew 26:64), and warned His disciples that they would preach an unpopular Gospel to the rulers: *"But beware of men; for they will deliver you up to the courts, and scourge you in their synagogues; and you shall even be brought before governors and kings for My sake, as a testimony to them and to the Gentiles"* (Matthew 10:17-18). Moreover, *"this Gospel of the Kingdom shall be preached in the whole world for a witness to all the nations, and then the end shall come"* (Matthew 24:14). And this was the Gospel order – to the Jews first, and then to the Gentiles (Acts 3:26; 11:18; 13:46-48; 28:23-29; Romans 1:16; 2:9): The angel preaches to the rulers of Palestine, and then to every nation and tribe and tongue and people. Before the end came in A.D. 70, Apostle Paul tells us, the Gospel was indeed preached to all the world (Romans 1:8; 10:18;

Colossians 1:5-6, 23). In spite of the attempts of the dragon and his two beasts to thwart the progress of the Gospel, the mission of the Apostles, Evangelists, martyrs, and confessors of the early Church was successful. The world was evangelized[55]

Another angel, a second one follows, presenting another aspect of the early Church's proclamation: Fallen, fallen is Babylon the Great! This is the first mention of "Babylon" in Revelation, a proleptic reference foreshadowing the full exposition to come in later chapters (similar to the early reference to the beast in Revelation 11:7). It is certainly possible, however, that Apostle John's readers understood his meaning immediately. In his first epistle, presumably written before the Revelation, Apostle Peter described the local church from which he wrote as "she who is in Babylon" (l Peter 5:13). Many have supposed this to be Rome, where Apostle Peter was (according to tradition) later martyred; but it is much more likely that the Apostle was in Jerusalem when he wrote these words. Based on data from the New Testament itself, our natural assumption should be that "Babylon" was Jerusalem, since that was where he lived and exercised his ministry (Acts 8:1; 12:3; Galatians 1:18; 2:1-9; cf. 1 Peter 4:17). Moreover, Apostle Peter's first epistle also sends greetings from Mark and Silas [Silvanus] (1 Pet. 5:12-13), both of whom lived in Jerusalem (Acts 12:12; 15:22-40).[56]

And another angel, a third one, followed them, with an appropriate message of doom for anyone who worships the beast and his image, or receives a mark in his forehead or upon his hand (see Revelation 13:15-18). The great offense of the land beast – apostate Israel's religious leadership – was the promotion and enforcement of the worship of the beast (Revelation 13:11-17). Apostle John is thus giving a clue to the great city's identity by repeating his words about the land beast immediately after his first statement about "Babylon." He is also reminding the Christians, especially the "angels," the Church officers, of their duty in proclaiming the whole counsel of God. They must preach the uncompromising message of the exclusive, all-encompassing lordship of Jesus Christ against all pretenders to the Throne. They must speak prophetically to their generation, sternly condemning the worship of

---

[55] See David Chilton, *Paradise Restored: A Biblical Theology of Dominion* (Ft. Worth, TX: Dominion Press, 1985), pp. 90f.

[56] For further material on the meaning of St. Peter's reference to "Baby- lon," see J. Stuart Russell, *The Parousia*, pp. 346ff.

the beast, warning that those who drink of Babylon's heretical cup of state-worship will also drink of the wine of the wrath of God, which is mixed in full strength – literally, mixed unmixed (or, as one commentator delightfully translates it, mixed neat[57]) – in the cup of His anger. The warning is clear: You cannot drink one cup without the other.

[58]THE GREAT HARVEST: REVELATION 14:14-20

> *Then I looked, and lo, a white cloud, and seated on the cloud one like a son of man, with a golden crown on his head, and a sharp sickle in his hand. And another angel came out of the temple, calling with a loud voice to him who sat upon the cloud, "Put in your sickle, and reap, for the hour to reap has come, for the harvest of the earth is fully ripe." So he who sat upon the cloud swung his sickle on the earth, and the earth was reaped. And another angel came out of the temple in heaven, and he too had a sharp sickle. Then another angel came out from the altar, the angel who has power over fire, and he called with a loud voice to him who had the sharp sickle, "Put in your sickle, and gather the clusters of the vine of the earth, for its grapes are ripe." So the angel swung his sickle on the earth and gathered the vintage of the earth, and threw it into the great wine press of the wrath of God; and the wine press was trodden outside the city, and blood flowed from the wine press, as high as a horse's bridle, for one thousand six hundred stadia.*

A lot of Prophets and preachers declare there will be a great end-time harvest of souls, with billions being swept into the Kingdom of God. While I am for this idea and would love to see it happen, I also realize they are declaring this based on a misinterpretation of Revelation 14. While I agree that the Kingdom of God will continue growing and expanding and filling the whole earth (see Daniel 2; Matthew 13:31–33), I also know Revelation 14 is not about an "end-time" revival. Revelation 14:17–20 speaks of the Harvester Angels reaping a harvest, which is thrown into the winepress of God's wrath, not into a revival! If we back up and look

---

[57] Carrington, pp. 248f. With the British sense of propriety, Carrington admits to a certain degree of trepidation in this rendering.
[58] Welton, Jonathan. Raptureless: An Optimistic Guide to the End of the World - Revised Edition Including The Art of Revelation. BookBaby. Kindle Edition.

at a parallel declaration from Jesus, this will begin to make sense. In Matthew 13, Jesus spoke of the approaching harvest. Jesus even indicated it would happen at the end of the age (aion), which was at AD 70.

Matthew 13:37-40
He answered, "He who sows the good seed is the Son of man; the field is the world, and the good seed means the sons of the kingdom; the weeds are the sons of the evil one, and the enemy who sowed them is the devil; the harvest is the close of the age, and the reapers are angels. Just as the weeds are gathered and burned with fire, so will it be at the close of the age.

Jesus spoke of good seed and bad seed. Revelation 14:4 speaks of the Christians as the first fruits, the good seed. In Revelation 14:14–20, it speaks of the bad seed being harvested and judged. Thus, in neither Matthew 13 nor Revelation 14 can we find proof of an end of the world harvest of souls! [End of quote.[59]]

In the beginning, when God created the earth, He gave breath/Spirit to His Image [Adam] and placed him in His garden-temple (Genesis 2:7-8); and the first thing we see the Image doing is *speaking,* naming and defining the creation in terms of God's mandate (Genesis 2:19-20).

The beast's spirit-inspired Image itself is able to cause as many as do not worship the image of the beast to be killed. The Jewish synagogues enforced submission to the Emperor. Indeed, their leaders' charge against Jesus Christ Himself was that He was a rival to the all-embracing authority of Caesar (John 19:12-15). Similarly, they organized economic boycotts against those who refused to submit to Caesar as Lord, the leaders of the synagogues "forbidding all dealings with the excommunicate,"[60] and going so far as to put them to death.

And he causes all, (note the six categories):

- the small and the great, and
- the rich and the poor, and
- the freemen and the slaves,

---

[59] *Ibid.*
[60] Austin Farrer, *The Revelation of St. John the Divine* (London: Oxford University Press, 1964), p. 157.

To be given a mark on their right hand, or on their forehead, and he provides that no one should be able to buy or to sell, except the one who has the mark, either the name of the beast or the number of his name. The Book of Acts is studded with incidents of organized Jewish persecution of the Church (Acts 4:1-3, 15-18; 5:17-18, 27-33, 40; 6:8-15; 7:51-60; 9:23, 29; 13:45-50; 14:2-5; 17:5-8, 13; 18:17; 20:3; 22:22-23; 23:12, 20-21; 24:27; 26:21; 28:17-29; cf. 1 Thessalonians 2:14-16). All of this ultimately served the interests of Caesar against Jesus Christ and His Church; and the *"mark of the beast,"* of course, is the satanic parody of the **"seal of God"** on the foreheads and hands of the righteous (Revelation 3:12; 7:2-4; 14:1), the mark of wholehearted obedience to the Law in thought and deed (Deuteronomy 6:6-8), the mark of blessing and protection (Ezekiel 9:4-6), the sign that one is *HOLY TO THE LORD* (cf. Exodus 28:36). Israel has rejected Jesus Christ and is "marked" with the seal of Rome's total lordship; she has given her allegiance to Caesar and is obedient to his rule and law. Israel chose to be saved by the pagan state and persecuted those who sought salvation in Christ.

There is a grim contrast here: The worshipers of the Beast, and those who receive his mark, have no rest day and night from their torments. The words are repeated from the description of the cherubim in Revelation 4:8, who have no rest day and night, eternally engaged in a sacrifice of praise.

Apostle John has just revealed the evil triad of enemies facing the early Church: **the dragon, the sea beast, and the land beast**. He has made it clear that these enemies are implacable, that the conflict with them will require faithfulness unto death. The question again naturally arises: Will the Church survive such an all-out attack?

In our next chapter we will begin our look into the seven last plagues.

CHAPTER EIGHT
SEVEN LAST PLAGUES

THE SONG OF VICTORY REVELATION 15:1-4

> *Then I saw another portent in heaven, great and wonderful, seven angels with seven plagues, which are the last, for with them the wrath of God is ended. And I saw what appeared to be a sea of glass mingled with fire, and those who had conquered the beast and its image and the number of its name, standing beside the sea of glass with harps of God in their hands. And they sing the song of Moses, the servant of God, and the song of the Lamb, saying, "Great and wonderful are thy deeds, O Lord God the Almighty! Just and true are thy ways, O King of the ages Who shall not fear and glorify thy name, O Lord? For thou alone art holy. All nations shall come and worship thee, for thy judgments have been revealed.*

Again, remember all this is taking place in the First Century. This is not a prophecy for our distant, distant future. No, the Apostle John was told by Jesus that these things were shortly [soon] to come to pass at the time of his writing prior to AD 70 when the Temple was to fall.

Then in verses 7-8 we see the following: Revelation 15:5-8

> *After this I looked, and the temple of the tent of witness in heaven was opened, and out of the temple came the seven angels with the*

seven plagues, robed in pure bright linen, and their breasts girded with golden girdles. And one of the four living creatures gave the seven angels seven golden bowls full of the wrath of God who lives for ever and ever; and the temple was filled with smoke from the glory of God and from his power, and no one could enter the temple until the seven plagues of the seven angels were ended.

We should be reminded in this context of the purification offering, designed to atone for the defilement of a *place,* so that God could continue to dwell with His people (cf. comments on Revelation 9:13). If the whole nation sinned, so that the entire Land was de- filed, the priests were required to perform special rites of purification: The blood of the sacrifice was sprinkled seven times to- ward the veil before the Holy of Holies, then smeared on the four horns of the altar, and the remainder poured out at the foot of the altar (Leviticus 4:13-21).[61] But in the outpoured plagues of the Chalice-judgments, this is reversed, as Philip Carrington points out: "This Blood, instead of bringing reconciliation, brings rejection and vengeance. Instead of being sprinkled seven times towards the veil, it is poured seven times on the Land. Instead of the appearance of the High Priest with the blood of reconciliation, we have Seven Angels with the Blood of Vengeance."[62]

Why is the blood in Revelation no longer sprinkled toward the veil? Because Jesus' blood has already been offered, and Israel has rejected it. So now it is time for the judgement of Israel, and this is what the Revelation is mainly about. After Israel is judged and the Temple destroyed the wrath of God would be finished and He would now be seeking to have His Kingdom extended to all nations, through the finished work of His son Jesus Christ. The Law and the Prophets of the Old Covenant age would be coming to an end, and everything would now be seen through the eyes and finished work of His Son.

Remember the account of Jesus' transfiguration in Matthew 17:1-8

And after six days Jesus took with him Peter and James and John his brother, and led them up a high mountain apart. And he was transfigured before them, and his face shone like the sun, and his

---

[61] See Gordon J. Wenham, *The Book of Leviticus* (Grand Rapids: William B. Eerdmans Publishing Co., 1979), pp. 86-103.
[62] Philip Carrington, *The Meaning of the Revelation* (London: SPCK, 1931), p. 262.

garments became white as light. And behold, there appeared to them Moses and Eli'jah, talking with him. And Peter said to Jesus, "Lord, it is well that we are here; if you wish, I will make three booths here, one for you and one for Moses and one for Eli'jah." He was still speaking, when lo, a bright cloud overshadowed them, and a voice from the cloud said, "This is my beloved Son, with whom I am well pleased; listen to him." When the disciples heard this, they fell on their faces, and were filled with awe. But Jesus came and touched them, saying, "Rise, and have no fear." And when they lifted up their eyes, they saw no one but Jesus only.

It is very interesting that Jesus would go up to this mountain and was transfigured before the eyes of His early Apostles. The word transfigure according to the English dictionary means:

- To give a new and typically exalted or spiritual appearance to.
- To transform outwardly and usually for the better

In Greek it is:

- **Strong's #3339:** metamorphoo (pronounced met-am-or-fo'-o) from 3326 and 3445; to transform (literally or figuratively, "metamorphose"): -change, transfigure, transform.
- **Thayer's Greek Lexicon:** metamorphoō
- To change into another form, to transform, to transfigure
- Christ appearance was changed and was resplendent with divine brightness on the mount of transfiguration

And as He reveals His full glory to a select group of His early Apostles they were completely blown away and wanted to stay upon the mountain because both Moses [the representative of the Old Covenant Law] and Elijah [the representative of the Old Covenant Prophets] were present with Jesus, even though they were both dead, they came back to life before the Apostles' very eyes. Jesus steps in and touches His Apostles letting them know that there was no longer any need for the Old Covenant representatives because He had fulfilled all the requirements of the Law and Prophets and had the power to take His rightful place in God's eternal plan for the human race. That they no longer would have to go this route but only had to come through the Finished Work of Jesus Christ and Him only. Hallelujah!

So now these seven Angels with the last plagues are about to bring eternal judgement on disobedient Israel. That is precisely Apostle John's point here: Blood and fire are about to be poured out upon the Land of Israel from the Seven Chalices, which are full of the wrath of God, who lives forever and ever. Indeed, God's eternal nature *("As I live forever!")* was given in the Song of Moses as a pledge of His vengeance against His enemies, and those who shed the blood of His servants (Deuteronomy 32:40-43). Thus we are shown that the seven Angels with the plagues come from *the Tabernacle of the Testimony,* bearing in their hands the curses of the Covenant; they come from the *Temple,* ['the Church'], as Ministers binding on earth the decrees of Heaven against those who have rejected the Testimony of Jesus; and they come from *the Throne of God* Himself, having received their Chalices of wrath from one of the Cherubs who carry God's Throne.

I like David Chilton's summary in his book "The Days of Vengeance":

With the coming of the New Covenant, the Church of Jesus Christ became the Temple of God. This new redemptive event was signaled by the Spirit's filling the Church on the Day of Pentecost, as He had filled the Tabernacle and the Temple. As St. Peter declared, however, the Pentecostal outpouring would be accompanied at the end of the age by a Holocaustal outpouring as well: "Blood, and fire, and vapor of smoke" (Acts 2:16-21; cf. Joel 2:28-32). For the Church to take full possession of her inheritance, for her to assume her proper place as the New Covenant Temple, the corrupt scaffold of the Old Covenant had to be thrown down and demolished. The first-generation Christians were continually exhorted to look forward to the fast-approaching Day when their adversaries would be consumed, and the Church "synagogued" as the definitive Temple (cf. 2 Thessalonians 2:1; Hebrews 10:25). In the complete sense of New Covenant fullness and "perfection" (cf. 1 Corinthians 13:12), no one was able to enter the Temple until the seven plagues of the seven angels were finished in the destruction of Old Covenant Israel.

The Seventh Trumpet was the sign that "there shall be no more delay" (cf. 10:6-7). Time has run out; wrath to the utmost has now come upon Israel. From this point on, Apostle John abandons the language and imagery of warning, concentrating wholly on the message of Jerusalem's impending destruction. As he describes the City's doom, he extends and intensifies the Exodus imagery that has already been so pervasive throughout the prophecy. Again, he mentions *"the Great City"* (Revelation 16:19), reminding his readers of a previous reference: *"the Great City, which Spiritually is called Sodom and Egypt, where also their Lord was crucified"* (Revelation 11:8). Jerusalem is called Sodom because of its sensual, luxurious apostasy (cf. Ezekiel 16:49-50), and because it is devoted to total destruction as a whole burnt sacrifice (Genesis 19:24-28; Deuteronomy 13:12-18). [End of quote from David Chilton's Days of Vengeance].

As we move into chapter 16, we get more details of the seven chalices of wrath given to the seven Angels.

Revelation 16:1-9
Then I heard a loud voice from the temple telling the seven angels, "Go and pour out on the earth the seven bowls of the wrath of God." So the first angel went and poured out his bowl on the earth; and a harmful and painful sore afflicted the people who had the mark of the beast and who worshiped his image. The second angel poured out his bowl into the sea, and it became blood like that of a dead man; and every living thing in the sea died. Then the third angel poured out his bowl into the rivers and the springs of waters; and they became blood. And I heard the angel of the waters saying, "Righteous are You, the One who is and who was, O Holy One, because You judged these things; for they poured out the blood of saints and prophets, and You have given them blood to drink. They deserve it." And I heard the altar saying, "Yes, Lord God, the Almighty, true and righteous are Your judgments." And the fourth angel poured out his bowl upon the sun, and it was given power to scorch people with fire. And the people were scorched with fierce heat; and they blasphemed the name of God who has the power over these plagues, and they did not repent so as to give Him glory.

The question that needs to be answered as we go deeper into these seven last plagues of the Revelation is this: What would the First Century Jew think and understand about these last plagues? Here is what I believe they would think.

As they read, about the plagues of Revelation 15–16, they would have immediately recalled the only other biblical occurrence of plagues, which came in the form of judgment against them—see Exodus 7–11.

In fact, as we dig a bit deeper in these last plagues, we will find some stunning direct parallels between the two lists of plagues. For example, the second and third bowls are about water turning to blood, which happened to the Nile during the plagues of Egypt (see Exod. 7:20). And the fifth bowl covers the land with darkness just like the ninth plague of Egypt (see Exodus 10:21-29).

In the Exodus account, the Egyptian armies pursued the Hebrews to the Red Sea, and the water swallowed them up, so the Hebrews were delivered. Yet in the sixth bowl judgment, ironically, an army rises from the river and brings destruction. In other words, the basic concept in Revelation 15–16 is a clear reversal of the Exodus story.

If you would remember, Revelation 11:8 [*And their dead bodies will lie on the street of the great city which spiritually is called Sodom and Egypt, where also their Lord was crucified.*] told us that God saw First Century Jerusalem as being like Egypt and Sodom. Later, we see the Christians make an exodus out of Jerusalem, as represented by the 144,000 who are marked by the Lord (see Revelation chapters 7 and 14). *Historically, we know that all the Christians fled Jerusalem and found safety in the nearby mountain of Pella, hence we can ascertain that none of the Christians were killed in the destruction of Jerusalem. As the Christians left, behind them was Jerusalem engulfed in the plagues that were sent by God.* This is the big picture of the bowls. Now Jerusalem has become like Egypt, and God is pouring out plagues upon it. Simply incredible!

> * Please understand, that Saints—the followers of Jesus Christ did die before the fall of the Temple as many were martyred. The ones I am referring to here, are the ones that fled the city just before the Temple and Jerusalem were destroyed. They heeded the prophetic warnings given by Jesus about 40 years before.

Here is a very important point for us to understand: notice here that the Christians sing the song of Moses. Now this was the same song that the Hebrews sang right after they were delivered from Egypt and the Egyptian army was killed in the Red Sea. In Revelation 15, the Christians sing the song of Moses as they are delivered from the new Egypt, First Century Jerusalem. That is what John was conveying to his readers.

Revelation 15:5-8
After this I looked, and the temple of the tent of witness in heaven was opened, and out of the temple came the seven angels with the seven plagues, robed in pure bright linen, and their breasts girded with golden girdles. And one of the four living creatures gave the seven angels seven golden bowls full of the wrath of God who lives for ever and ever; and the temple was filled with smoke from the glory of God and from his power, and no one could enter the temple until the seven plagues of the seven angels were ended.

"The judgments of the vials are the overflow of the wrath of God blazing forth and filling His Temple, a visitation or presence vouchsafed in response to the prayers of His Saints."[63]

As the first angel pours out his Chalice into the Land, it becomes ***a loathsome and malignant sore upon the men who had the mark of the Beast and who worshiped his image.*** The sores are a fitting retribution for apostasy, "a hideous stamp avenging the mark of the beast.[64]

The second Angel pours out his Chalice into the sea, and it becomes blood, as in the first Egyptian plague (Exodus 7:17-21) and the Second Trumpet (Revelation 8:8-9). This time, however, the blood is not running in streams, but instead is **like that of a dead man**: clotted, coagulated, and putrefying. Blood is mentioned four times in this chapter; it covers the face of Israel, spilling over the four corners of the Land.

The third Angel pours out of the third Chalice, and it more directly resembles the first Egyptian plague (and the third Trumpet: cf. Revelation 8:10-11), since it affects the rivers and the springs of waters, turning all the drinking water to blood. Water is a symbol of life and blessing throughout

---

[63] Austin Farrer, *The Revelation of St. John the Divine* (Oxford: At the Clarendon Press, 1964), p. 175.
[64] Ibid., p. 175.

Scripture, beginning from the story of creation and the Garden of Eden.[65] In this plague, the blessings of Paradise are reversed and turned into a nightmare; what was once pure and clean becomes polluted and unclean through apostasy.

The fourth Angel pours out his Chalice upon the sun, and it was given to it to scorch the men with fire. Whereas the fourth Trumpet resulted in a plague of darkness (Revelation 8:12), now the heat of the sun is increased, so that the men were scorched with great heat. This too is a reversal of a basic covenantal blessing that was present in the Exodus, when Israel was shielded from the heat of the sun by the Glory-Cloud, the Shadow of the Almighty (Exodus 13:21-22; cf. Psalms 91:1-6). This promise is repeated again and again throughout the Prophets: See Psalms 121:5-7; Isaiah 49:10 and Jeremiah 17:7-8.

But the apostates refuse to submit to God's lordship over them. Like the Beast, whose head is crowned with *"names of blasphemy"* (Revelation 13:1) and whose image they worship, the men blasphemed the name of God who has the power over these plagues. And, like the impenitent Pharaoh (cf. Exodus 7:13, 23; 8:15, 19, 32; 9:7, 12, 34-35; 10:20, 27; 11:10; 14:8), they did not repent so as to give Him glory. Israel has become an Egypt, hardening its heart; and, like Egypt, it is being destroyed.

On to the last three Chalices It Is Finished: Revelation 16:10-21

> *The fifth angel poured his bowl on the throne of the beast, and its kingdom was in darkness; men gnawed their tongues in anguish and cursed the God of heaven for their pain and sores, and did not repent of their deeds. The sixth angel poured his bowl on the great river Euphra'tes, and its water was dried up, to prepare the way for the kings from the east. And I saw, issuing from the mouth of the dragon and from the mouth of the beast and from the mouth of the false prophet, three foul spirits like frogs; for they are demonic spirits, performing signs, who go abroad to the kings of the whole world, to assemble them for battle on the great day of God the Almighty. ("Lo, I am coming like a thief! Blessed is he who is awake, keeping his garments that he may not go naked and be seen exposed!") And they assembled them at the place which is called*

---

[65] David Chilton, *Paradise Restored: A Biblical Theology of Dominion* (Ft. Worth, TX: Dominion Press, 1985), pp. 18lf, 30f.

> in Hebrew Armaged'don. The seventh angel poured his bowl into the air, and a loud voice came out of the temple, from the throne, saying, "It is done!" And there were flashes of lightning, voices, peals of thunder, and a great earthquake such as had never been since men were on the earth, so great was that earthquake. The great city was split into three parts, and the cities of the nations fell, and God remembered great Babylon, to make her drain the cup of the fury of his wrath. And every island fled away, and no mountains were to be found; and great hailstones, heavy as a hundredweight, dropped on men from heaven, till men cursed God for the plague of the hail, so fearful was that plague.

Although most of the judgments throughout Revelation are aimed specifically at apostate Israel, the heathen who joined Israel against the Church came under condemnation as well. Indeed, the Great Tribulation itself would prove to be "the hour of testing, that hour, which was to come upon *the whole world,* to test those who dwell upon *the Land"* (Revelation 3:10). The fifth angel therefore pours out his Chalice **upon the throne of the beast;** and, even as the sun's heat is scorching those who worship the beast, the lights are turned out on **his kingdom,** and it becomes **darkened—**a familiar Biblical symbol for political turmoil and the fall of rulers (cf. Isaiah 13:9-10; Amos 8:9; Ezekiel 32:7-8).

It is also likely, however, that this judgment partially corresponds to the wars, revolutions, riots, and "world-wide convulsions"[66] that racked the Empire after Nero committed suicide in June 68. F. W. Farrar writes in this connection of "the horrors inflicted upon Rome and Romans in the civil wars by provincial governors—already symbolized as the horns of the wild beast, and here characterized as kings yet kingdomless. Such were Galba, Otho, Vitellius, and Vespasian.

[67]In the sixth bowl, the armies of Rome come from the Euphrates River. We also see mention of Jesus coming in judgment like a thief in the night. In other words, the attack upon Jerusalem would come when no one expected it, and the Christians would need to be alert to escape before the city was surrounded and escape became impossible. Jesus first talks about this in Matthew 24:42–44:

---

[66] Cornelius Tacitus, *The Histories,* iii.49.
[67] Welton, Jonathan. The Art of Revelation. BookBaby. Kindle Edition.

Watch therefore, for you do not know on what day your Lord is coming. But know this, that if the householder had known in what part of the night the thief was coming, he would have watched and would not have let his house be broken into. Therefore you also must be ready; for the Son of man is coming at an hour you do not expect. [End of quote].

Again, this Sixth bowl was poured out upon the great river, the Euphrates; and its water was dried up, that the way might be prepared for the kings from the rising of the sun. As we saw in Revelation 9:14, the Euphrates was Israel's northern frontier, from which invading armies would come to ravage and oppress the Covenant people. The image of the drying of the Euphrates for a conquering army is taken, in part, from a stratagem of Cyrus the Persian, who conquered Babylon by temporarily turning the Euphrates out of its course, enabling his army to march up the riverbed into the city, taking it by surprise. the drying up of the Red Sea (Exodus 14:21-22) and the Jordan River (Joshua 3:9-17; 4:22-24) for the victorious people of God. Again, there is the underlying note of tragic irony: Israel has become the new Babylon, an enemy of God that must now be conquered by a new Cyrus, as the true Covenant people are miraculously delivered and brought into their inheritance. As Carrington observes, the coming of the armies from the Euphrates "surely represents nothing but the return of Titus to besiege Jerusalem with further reinforcements";[68] and it is certainly more than coincidental that thousands of these very troops actually did come from the Euphrates.[69]

In the seventh bowl, Jerusalem which is divided into three sections receives a torrent of great hailstones falling. Ancient Jerusalem consisted of three successively higher sections. During the Roman invasion, the Roman army captured the city in three stages, first destroying the lowest section before laying siege to the next section and then finally the third section. In this way, the city was divided into three parts. The hailstones mentioned in the seventh bowl weighed one talent. The heavy common talent, used in New Testament times, was 58.9 kg (129 lb 14 oz). Josephus records that the Roman armies lobbed white limestones weighing exactly one talent from their catapults, thus destroying the defenses of Jerusalem in what would have appeared to be a hailstorm of white rocks

---

[68] Philip Carrington, *The Meaning of the Revelation* (London: SPCK, 1930, p. 265.
[69] See Josephus, *The Jewish War,* ii.Li.3; iii.iv.2; v.i.6; vii.i.3.

weighing the exact amount recorded in John's prophecy. Josephus writes: The stone missiles weighed a talent and traveled two furlongs or more, and their impact not only on those who were hit first, but also on those behind them, was enormous. At first the Jews kept watch for the stone— for it was white—and its approach was intimated to the eye by its shining surface as well as to the ear by its whizzing sound.[70]

If we keep in mind that the Old Covenant was the veil and that the removal of the veil was the revealing or revelation of Jesus Christ, then we can look upon this traumatic time—when the old covenant world was being stoned to death for its unfaithfulness to its covenant partner—with gladness that we live fully in the new covenant. We are in a New Covenant of forgiveness that contains no wrath. As Revelation 15:1 says: *"Then I saw another sign in heaven, great and amazing, seven angels with seven plagues, which are the last, for with them the wrath of God is finished"* (ESV).

And Paul writes similarly:

For you, brethren, became imitators of the churches of God in Christ Jesus that are in Judea, for you also endured the same sufferings at the hands of your own countrymen, even as they did from the Jews, who both killed the Lord Jesus and the prophets, and drove us out. They are not pleasing to God, but hostile to all men, hindering us from speaking to the Gentiles so that they may be saved; with the result that they always fill up the measure of their sins. But wrath has come upon them to the utmost (NASB 1 Thessalonians 2:14–16).

The bowls containing the last of the plagues have been poured out; but the end is not yet. The chapters that follow will close in on the destruction of the great harlot-City and her allies and conclude with the revelation of the glorious Bride of Christ: the true Holy City, New Jerusalem.

God poured out His wrath upon the Old Covenant until it was no more, and then He welcomed us into the New Covenant of forgiveness, which contains no wrath at all.

In our next chapter we would be looking at and deconstructing the meaning of the "false bride".

---

[70] Quoted in David Chilton, Days of Vengeance (Dallas, GA: Dominion Press, 1987), 417.

CHAPTER NINE
THE FALSE BRIDE

WHILE SOME IN RECENT YEARS HAVE ATTEMPTED TO SEE THE GREAT HARLOT OF Revelation as the City of Rome, the Church throughout Christian history has generally understood that she is in some sense a false bride, a demonic parody of the True Bride, the Church.

After explaining the bowls of wrath, John paints Revelation's most mysterious symbol—Babylon the harlot. Many wild theories have surfaced regarding the harlot, but they have overlooked an incredible clue within the book that will help us interpret the symbols of Sodom, Babylon, and the harlot. That clue is the reoccurring term the Great City. In its first occurrence, the text tells us that the Great City is figuratively called Sodom and Egypt, yet literally speaking, this was the city where Jesus was crucified. Therefore, the Great City is Jerusalem. *"Their bodies will lie in the public square of the great city—which is figuratively called Sodom and Egypt—where also their Lord was crucified"* (Revelation 11:8). With this key in hand, we can begin to see that Revelation 16–18 speaks of the First Century Jerusalem as not only Sodom and Egypt but also as Babylon the great harlot that fornicated with the kings of the earth. After all, the Jews said at Jesus' trial, *"We have no king but Caesar!"* (John 19:15), firmly rejecting their Messiah, their Bridegroom, and joining themselves in adultery with the Roman government.[71]

---

[71] Welton, Jonathan. The Art of Revelation. BookBaby. Kindle Edition.

The Biblical *motif* of the Bride falling into adultery (apostasy) is so well-known that such an identification is all but inescapable. The metaphor of harlotry is exclusively used in the Old Testament for a city or nation that has abandoned the Covenant and turned toward false gods; and, with only two exceptions (see in verses 1-2, below), the term is always used for faithless Israel. The Harlot is clearly the false church.

We have seen that the Book of Revelation presents us with two great cities, set in antithesis to each other: *Babylon* and *New Jerusalem.* As we shall see in a later chapter, the New Jerusalem is Paradise Consummated, the community of the saints, the City of God. The other city, which is continually contrasted to the New Jerusalem, is the *old* Jerusalem, which has become unfaithful to God. Another way to view this is to understand that Jerusalem was intended from the beginning to be the true fulfillment of *Babylon,* a word meaning "Gate of God." The place of God's gracious revelation of Himself and of His Covenant should be a true Babylon, a true "Gate of Heaven" and "House of God," as Jacob understood when he saw God's staircase to heaven, the true Tower of Babel. Like the original Babylon, Jerusalem turned its back on the true God and sought autonomous glory and dominion. Like the original Babylon, it was apostate; and thus the "Gate of God" became "Confusion" instead (Genesis 11:9).[72]

The Identity of the harlot: Revelation 17:1-7

> *Then one of the seven angels who had the seven bowls came and said to me, "Come, I will show you the judgment of the great harlot who is seated upon many waters, with whom the kings of the earth have committed fornication, and with the wine of whose fornication the dwellers on earth have become drunk." And he carried me away in the Spirit into a wilderness, and I saw a woman sitting on a scarlet beast which was full of blasphemous names, and it had seven heads and ten horns. The woman was arrayed in purple and scarlet, and bedecked with gold and jewels and pearls, holding in her hand a golden cup full of abominations and the impurities of her fornication; and on her forehead was written a name of mystery: "Babylon the great, mother of harlots and of earth's abominations." And I saw the woman, drunk with the blood of the saints and the blood of the martyrs of Jesus. When I saw her I marveled greatly.*

---

[72] Quoted in David Chilton, Days of Vengeance (Dallas, GA: Dominion Press, 1987), 422.

> *But the angel said to me, "Why marvel? I will tell you the mystery of the woman, and of the beast with seven heads and ten horns that carries her.*

The harlot-city has committed fornication with the kings of the earth. This expression is taken from Isaiah's prophecy against Tyre, where it primarily refers to her international commerce (Isa. 23:15-17); Nineveh as well is accused of "many harlotries" with other nations (Nahum 3:4).

Some commentators have suggested that both the beast from the sea and Babylon the harlot are Rome. However, this does not seem to be a plausible option for several reasons. While it is clear that the beast from the sea represents Rome, it is also equally clear that the Babylonian harlot city is not Rome. Here are three reasons why:

1. The harlot rides the beast (see Revelation 17:3). It does not make sense that Rome would ride on Rome.
2. The beast hates the harlot and destroys her with fire (see Revelation 17:16). Rome did not hate Rome and destroy Rome with fire.
3. If the beast and the harlot are both Rome, it does not make sense that the beast would wage war on Jesus after the harlot is destroyed. In Revelation 18:21-24 Babylon, the harlot city, is destroyed. Yet, in the next chapter, in Revelation 19:19-21, the beast gathers to wage war against Jesus, but is thrown into the lake of fire.

Interpreting the beast from the sea as Rome is completely reasonable and logical, and most commentators have chosen this interpretation over the course of Church history. But to say that the Great City—Babylon the harlot—is also Rome is unreasonable once we examine the interactions between the beast and the harlot. They absolutely cannot both refer to Rome.[73] Revelation 17:9 reads: *"The seven heads are seven hills on which the woman [harlot] sits."* Yet, the seven hills are not used to identify the Babylonian harlot, but the beast. It is the beast that has seven symbolic

---

[73] Some commentators, especially Historicists, will make a half leap into Idealism and say that the harlot that rides the beast is the Roman Catholic Church, or in more general terms, the "evil spirit or principality of religion." This would mean that the beast [Rome] hated the principality behind Rome and burned the principality with fire. Then after the principality fell (not because of God, but because Rome cast it down?!), the beast [Rome] was judged separately without an evil principality. This concept falls apart upon thoughtful consideration.

heads, which are seven hills. Rome is the city with seven hills in view here. Rome is the beast, and the Babylonian harlot rides on the beast with seven heads, which are seven hills (see Revelation 17:7, 9). Clearly, the harlot and the beast are two different characters.[74] Saying that the seven hills surround Rome does not identify the harlot as Rome.[75]

Incidentally, this is one of many indications that the Harlot is not Rome, for she is clearly distinct from it. She is *seated* on the beast, supported, and maintained by him whose seven heads represent - among other things - the famed "seven hills" of Rome (Revelation 17:9 *This calls for a mind with wisdom: the seven heads are seven mountains on which the woman is seated;*).

There is just so much one can draw from this last book of the Bible, but in this writing, I am seeking to cover as many of the main points as I can. Therefore, in our next chapter we would take a look at "The Marriage of The Lamb", where we would find out some very interesting facts according to the Scriptures. So, think deeply as we navigate this next chapter.

---

[74] For an explanation of why Babylon is symbolic of Jerusalem and the beast is symbolic of the Roman Empire, see Kenneth Gentry, Navigating the Book of Revelation (Fountain Inn, SC: GoodBirth Ministries, 2009), 141–149.
[75] Welton, Jonathan. The Art of Revelation. BookBaby. Kindle Edition.

CHAPTER TEN
MARRIAGE OF THE LAMB

I USED TO BELIEVE THE MARRIAGE SUPPER OF THE LAMB WAS A FAR DISTANT FUTURE event, but our only picture of the timing is in Revelation 19:7, *"Let us rejoice and be glad and give him glory! For the wedding of the Lamb has come, and his bride has made herself ready."* According to this verse, the marriage happened right after Heaven rejoiced over the AD 70 destruction of Jerusalem. It happened right before the beast, the false prophet, and those who took the mark of the beast were all judged in Revelation 19:11–21.

For many, this may require a shift in thinking. The Church is not currently a lonely fiancé withering away and wondering when her wedding will be. The Church is already married to Christ; we are in the New Covenant, and we remain in Him, and He remains in us (see John 15:4). In other words, the two have become one, and those who are joined to the Lord are one spirit with Him (see 1 Corinthians 6:17).

This means that our modern reality is not necessarily the same as that of the Christians prior to the destruction of Jerusalem. They were living in a unique forty-year transition time between the Cross and the destruction of Jerusalem. The New Covenant was established at the Cross, however, the Old Covenant still existed. The whole purpose of Jesus' coming in judgment in AD 70 was to completely and once and for all remove the Old Covenant and fully establish the New (see Hebrews 8:13). When this happened, the Christian reality changed for the better. On the other side of AD 70, we are not looking forward to Christ's coming and the 'end of the age'. We get to live in the current reality of His promises and the fullness of the New Covenant. Now tell me where am I wrong with this understanding?

We are now the Bride of Christ. We are not waiting for the marriage supper of the Lamb. We are already married to Him. However, the New Testament Believers were awaiting their marriage to Christ as part of His coming in AD 70. This becomes clear when we look at several statements in the New Testament and the Revelation sequence of events.

In Ephesians 5, when Paul compares earthly marriage to our union with Christ, he refers to the union of Christ and the Church as "a profound mystery" (Ephesians 5:32). The two are going to become one. However, in Romans 7:1–6, Paul says a woman cannot be married to another man while her first husband is still alive. This would make her an adulterer. Thus, her first husband must die, and then she will be free to marry the new husband. In saying this, he is illustrating what must happen so that the Church can be married spiritually to Christ. The first husband was the Old Covenant, and the new husband is Christ. So, for the Bride to marry Christ, her Old Covenant husband had to be first done away with.

During the First Century, the Church lived as betrothed to her new husband, Christ, but not yet married. In other words, there was a forty-year engagement period. Are you seeing this? I believe it makes complete sense. This is why, after the Revelation account of the AD 70 events, John then gives an account of the marriage supper of the Lamb. First the Old Covenant needed to be fully annulled. Then, the Church could be presented to Christ as His Bride. This is what Paul declared when he wrote, *"Whoever is united with the Lord is one with him in spirit"* (1 Corinthians 6:17).

Paul, writing before AD 70, writes as though the marriage has already taken place, as though the Church and Christ have already become one. This is because, in the Hebrew culture of his day, betrothal was just as binding as marriage.[76] However, the marriage actually happened in the events of Revelation 19. The first mention of the Bride is that she has

---

[76] "The formal betrothal may take place some years before the marriage. The bridegroom elect sends a present to the girl, the dowry is settled, and if sometime afterwards the engagement be broken off, the young woman, if a Jewess, cannot be married to anyone else without first a paper of divorce from the rabbi." G.M. Mackie, Bible Manners and Customs (Westwood, NJ: Barbour Books, 1991), 131.

prepared herself for the marriage: *"Let us rejoice and be glad and give him glory! For the wedding of the Lamb has come, and his bride has made herself ready"* (Revelation 19:7). This comes after the destruction of the Great City Babylon (Jerusalem) by the beast (the Roman Empire) in Revelation 17. The Roman Empire fought against the Jewish people in AD 70, but it also fought against God by persecuting the early Christians. Thus, as Jerusalem faces its destruction, Jesus calls His followers out from among the hardened Jews of Jerusalem: *"'Come out of her, my people,' so that you will not share in her sins, so that you will not receive any of her plagues"* (Revelation 18:4). This describes the historical event when the Christians in Jerusalem fled to Mount Pella, where they were spared from the destruction of AD 70.

After the fall of Jerusalem, the time for the marriage supper had finally come. All this is a picture of the union between Christ and the Church that John wrote about prophetically and that Paul stated beforehand, as though it had already taken place. Then, in conjunction with the destruction of Jerusalem and the end of the Old Covenant, the New Covenant marriage supper takes place.[77]

Now, we are on the other side of this marriage supper, and we are the Bride of Christ. The two have become one, and we are equally yoked. We are no longer married to the Law, but we are married to Christ in the New Covenant. Because of this, we are now His ambassadors, as co-heirs and co-rulers, to bring the Kingdom into the earth. As those living on the other side of AD 70, with all the inheritance and all the promises, we get to remake all things new together with Christ (see Revelation 21:5). He has overcome, and through Him, we too have overcome. Understanding this changes how we live. It's not just a revelation that certain events are in our past. It changes our understanding of our identity and purpose on earth. Hallelujah!

---

[77] In Matthew 22:1-7, Jesus says, "The kingdom of heaven is like a king who prepared a wedding banquet for his son. He sent his servants to those who had been invited to the banquet to tell them to come, but they refused to come. Then he sent some more servants and said, 'Tell those who have been invited that I have prepared my dinner: My oxen and fattened cattle have been butchered, and everything is ready. Come to the wedding banquet.' But they paid no attention and went off—one to his field, another to his business. The rest seized his servants, mistreated them and killed them. The king was enraged. He sent his army and destroyed those murderers and burned their city." Here, verse 7 connects the wedding of the son with the enraged king bringing justice and burning the city. The AD 70 destruction of Jerusalem and the marriage of the Son are unavoidably connected.

In the next chapter I would like for us to have a look what the thousand years referred to in Revelation 20.

CHAPTER ELEVEN
THE THOUSAND YEAR

REVELATION 20:1-3

> *Then I saw an angel coming down from heaven, holding in his hand the key of the bottomless pit and a great chain. And he seized the dragon, that ancient serpent, who is the devil and satan, and bound him for a thousand years, and threw him into the pit, and shut it and sealed it over him, that he should deceive the nations no more, till the thousand years were ended. After that he must be loosed for a little while.*

In dealing with the 1,000-year reign:

In a recorded sermon, Pastor Bill Johnson of Bethel Church in Redding, California, USA made some interesting observations about Revelation 20.

He said: We have statements in Scripture concerning the beasts and the thousand years. For example, it says that the dragon will be bound with chains and cast into a bottomless pit for a thousand years. Now I don't want to take away your millennium…

I just want to suggest that we might not know what we are talking about because there are only a couple of verses in the Bible on the subject!

Then Bill Johnson began asking questions of the audience:

Bill Johnson: The Dragon, literal or figurative? Is it a real dragon?

Audience replies: Figurative

Bill Johnson: The Chains, literal or figurative? Are they actual chains?
Audience replies: Figurative
Bill Johnson: The Bottomless pit, literal or figurative?
Audience replies: Figurative
Bill Johnson: The Millennium, literal or figurative?

To this question, the audience replies only with stunned silence. Bill then went on to speak about how we have allowed our interpretation of the millennium and other passages to cancel out our responsibility to demonstrate the Kingdom of God in the present—as if many of the Bible's promises are not for today. This point makes all the difference in how we live our Christian lives.

During the Millennium — I really like what Jonathan Welton said about this in his book "The Art of Revelation" as follows:

Now let's look at what the Bible says will happen during the millennium:

I saw thrones on which were seated those who had been given authority to judge. And I saw the souls of those who had been beheaded because of their testimony about Jesus and because of the word of God. They had not worshiped the beast or its image and had not received its mark on their foreheads or their hands. They came to life and reigned with Christ a thousand years (Revelation 20:4).

The English translation of this passage makes it seem like there are two groups of people in view here, yet in the Greek it is clear that John was describing one group of people, the same group from Revelation 6:9-11:

When he opened the fifth seal, I saw under the altar the souls of those who had been slain because of the word of God and the testimony they had maintained. They called out in a loud voice, "How long, Sovereign Lord, holy and true, until you judge the inhabitants of the earth and avenge our blood? "Then each of them was given a white robe, and they were told to wait a little longer, until the full number of their fellow servants, their brothers and sisters, were killed just as they had been."

In chapter 6, we find these martyrs under the throne crying out for justice, but in chapter 20, the same martyrs are given thrones of their own to reign in judgment upon! I know this because of the next verse: Revelation 20:5 NIV

(The rest of the dead did not come to life until the thousand years were ended.) This is the first resurrection.

This phrase, *"The rest of the dead,"* makes it clear that this group of people is a select number from among the dead. To find out what separates these ones who reign on thrones from *"the rest,"* we need to look at the passage right before chapter 20 begins:

But the beast was captured, and with it the false prophet who had performed the signs on its behalf. With these signs he had deluded those who had received the mark of the beast and worshiped its image. The two of them were thrown alive into the fiery lake of burning sulfur. The rest were killed with the sword coming out of the mouth of the rider on the horse, and all the birds gorged themselves on their flesh (Revelation 19:19-21).

The ones in question, *"The rest of the dead,"* were those who died in the AD 70 destruction, the non-believing Jews. We know this to be true because the time indicator in Revelation 19:20 tells us this happened at the same time as the destruction of the Beast and the false prophet, that is Nero and the Jewish Rulers.

Thus far, this is what we have found in Revelation 20:

A time period that is very long, symbolized by the number one thousand:

- First Century martyrs sitting on thrones and passing judgment
- First Century Jewish non-Believers being judged
- The dragon (devil) being bound in his ability to deceive the nations
  Importantly, we have not found any of the following popular ideas:
- A rebuilt temple in Jerusalem
- The reestablishment of the Old Covenant system
- Jesus reigning physically upon the earth

These concepts that are not found in Revelation 20 have been injected by the system Darby founded in the most abusive form of eisegesis (reading one's own ideas into a text). Darbyists construct their view of the thousand years by taking passages from Jeremiah, Zechariah, Ezekiel, and Isaiah and tearing them out of context in order to make them fit with Revelation 20.

If I were to simply paraphrase my understanding of Revelation 20, I would explain it this way: The thousand years represents the Kingdom of God. When Jesus came to earth, He bound the devil (the strong man, as in Matthew 12:28-29), and the devil could no longer deceive the nations (see Revelation 20:3). This paved the way for the disciples to disciple all nations (see Matthew 28:18-20). The First Century martyrs were given thrones to reign upon in the Kingdom; this occurred in Revelation 11, when Jesus was declared the King over the kingdoms of the earth (see Revelation 11:15) and the first resurrection was indicated (see Revelation 11:17-18). We now live inside the Kingdom of God on the earth, which is growing as the mustard seed and as the leaven going through the loaf (see Matthew 13:31-33). We are in the millennial reign, which is a spiritual Kingdom that is bringing Heaven into the earth progressively (see Matthew 6:10). Someday in the future, the Kingdom will have advanced so far that the only thing remaining to do will be to judge the devil finally and completely. He will be released from his chains to gather up whoever still resists the Kingdom, and the lot of them will be thrown into the lake of fire.[78]

It would have clearly shown his audience that it was about the forthcoming second destruction of Jerusalem in AD 70.

Let us now revisit the first few verses of Revelation 20, where we see that satan is bound and cast into the pit for a thousand years. Let us dig a bit deeper into this:

The importance of the imagery in this passage is heightened by its centrality as the fourth of seven visions introduced by the expression And I saw *(kai eidon;* cf. 19:11, 17, 19; 20:4, 11; 21:1). S1. John sees an Angel coming down from Heaven, having the key of the Abyss and a great chain in His hand. Again, as in Revelation 10:1 and 18:1 (cf. 12:7), this is the Lord Jesus Christ, who as Mediator is the Angel (Messenger) of the

---

[78] Welton, Jonathan. Raptureless: An Optimistic Guide to the End of the World - Revised Edition Including The Art of Revelation. BookBaby. Kindle Edition.

Covenant (Malachi 2:7; 3:1). His absolute control and authority over the Abyss are symbolized by the key and the great chain. The author sets up a striking contrast: satan, the evil star *that fell* from Heaven, was briefly *given* the key to the Abyss (Revelation 9:1); but Christ descended from Heaven, having as His lawful possession "the keys of death and of Hades" Revelation 1:18).

Apostle John brings together the various descriptions of the evil one that he has used throughout the prophecy: the Dragon (Revelation 2:3-4,7, 9, 13, 16-17; 13:2, 4, 11; 16:13), the serpent of old (Revelation 9:19; 12:9, 14-15), the devil (Revelation 2:10; 12:9, 12), satan (Revelation 2:9, 13, 24; 3:9; 12:9), the deceiver of the whole world (Revelation 2:20; 12:9; 13:14; 18:23; 19:20). But the terrifying power of this enemy only serves to display the surpassing greatness of his Conqueror, who has so easily rendered him impotent: Jesus Christ, in His mission as the *"Angel from heaven," laid hold of the Dragon. . . and bound* **him for a thousand years, and threw him into the pit** *or Abyss,* **and shut it and sealed it over him.** As Apostle John declared in his first epistle, *Christ "appeared for this purpose, that He might destroy the works of the devil"* (l John 3:8). In terms of this purpose, the Lord began "binding the strong man" during His earthly ministry; having successfully completed His mission, *He is now plundering satan's house and carrying off his property:*

Matthew 12:28-29 reveals this:

But if it is by the Spirit of God that I cast out demons, then the kingdom of God has come upon you. Or how can one enter a strong man's house and plunder his goods, unless he first binds the strong man? Then indeed he may plunder his house.

Herman Ridderbos comments on the significance of this statement and goes on to provide an excellent summary of the Gospel accounts of Christ's victory over the devil: "This passage [Matthew 12:28; Luke 11:20] is not an isolated one. The whole struggle of Jesus against the devils is determined by the antithesis between the Kingdom of Heaven and the rule of satan, and time and again Jesus' superior power over satan and satan's dominion proves the breakthrough on the part of the Kingdom of God. This is already proved at the start by the temptation in the wilderness. There can be no doubt that in it the issue is Jesus' messianic kingship.

Three times in succession it is satan's point of departure, referring back to the divine words about Jesus at His baptism (Matthew 3:17; Mark 1:11; Luke 3:22; Matthew 4:3, 6; Luke 4:3, 9). Especially the temptation with respect to *'all the kingdoms of the world'* (Matthew 4:8ff.; Luke 4:5ff.) shows what is at issue in the struggle between Jesus and satan. Here satan appears as *'the prince of the world'* (cf. John 12:31; 14:30; 16:11), who opposes God's Kingdom, and who knows that Jesus will dispute that power with him in the Name of God. Here, then, together with the Messiahship, the Kingdom of God is at issue. At the same time, it appears that the victory over satan to be gained by the Kingdom of God is not only a matter of *power,* but first and foremost one of *obedience* on the part of the Messiah. The Messiah must not make an arbitrary use of the authority entrusted to Him. He will have to acquire the power that satan offers Him only in the way ordained by God. That is why Jesus' rejection of the temptation is already the beginning of His victory and of the coming of the Kingdom, although this victory will have to be renewed again and again during His life on earth (cf. Luke 4:13; Matthew 16:23, and parallels; 26:38, and parallels; 27:40-43, and parallels).

From the beginning of His public activity Jesus' power over satan had already asserted itself. This is not only proved by the casting out of devils in itself, but also by *the manner in which those possessed by the devil behave in His presence* (cf. Mark 1:24; Luke 4:34; Mark 5:7; Matthew 8:29; Luke 8:28, 31). When Jesus approaches, they raise a cry, obviously in fear. They show that they have a supernatural knowledge of His person and of the significance of His coming (cf. Mark 1:34; 3:11). They call Him 'the Holy One of God,' 'the Son of God,' 'Son of the most high God.' By this they recognize His messianic dignity (cf. Luke 4:41). They consider His coming as their own destruction (Mark 1:24; Luke 4:34); their torment (Matthew 8:29; Mark 5:7; Luke 8:28). They feel powerless and try only to lengthen their existence on earth (Matthew 8:29; Mark 5:10) and implore Him not to send them into 'the deep,' that is to say, the place of their eternal woe (Luke 8:31, cf. Revelation 20:3ff.). All this shows that in Jesus' person and coming the Kingdom has become a present reality. For the exercise of God's power over the devil and his rule has the coming of the Kingdom for its foundation.

And finally, we must refer in this context to Luke 10:18-19. Jesus has sent out the seventy (or seventy-two) who come back to Him and joyfully told Him of the success of their mission. And then Jesus says: '*I beheld satan as lightning fall from heaven.*' Thus, He accepts the joy of those He had sent out and shows them the background of their power over the devils. The general meaning of this is clear: satan himself has fallen with great force from his position of power. This is what Jesus had seen with His own eyes. satan's supporters cannot maintain themselves. . .. The thing that counts in this connection is that what is said here is essentially the same thing as in Matthew 12:28 and Luke 11:20, ie., the great moment of the breaking down of satan's rule has come and at the same time that of the coming of the Kingdom of Heaven.

The redemption is no longer future but has become *present.* In this struggle it is Jesus Himself who has broken satan's power and who continues to do so. Such appears from what follows when He discusses the power of the disciples which they have received from Him to tread on serpents and scorpions and over all the power of the enemy, so that, in the future also, nothing will be impossible to them. By this *enemy* satan is again meant. *serpents* and *scorpions* are mentioned here as his instruments (Psalm 91:13) by which he treacherously tries to ruin man. But any power satan has at his disposal to bring death and destruction (cf., e.g., Hebrew 2:14) has been subjected to the disciples. All this implies and confirms that the great moment of salvation, the fulfillment of the promise, the Kingdom of Heaven, has come."[79]

The whole message of the New Testament (cf. Ephesians 4:8; Colossians 2:15; Hebrews 2:14) stresses that satan was definitively defeated in the life, death, resurrection, and ascension of Jesus Christ. It is absolutely crucial to remember that in speaking of Christ's "Ascension"- His Coming to the Throne of the Ancient of Days (Daniel 7:13-14)-we are speaking not only of His single act of ascending into the Cloud, but also of the direct and immediate consequences of that act: the outpouring of the Spirit on the Church in A.D. 30 (Luke 24:49-51; John 16:7; Acts 2:17-18, 33), and the outpouring of wrath upon Jerusalem and the Temple in A.D. 70 (Daniel 9:24-27; Acts 2:19-20). Pentecost and Holocaust were the Ascension applied. The final act in the drama of the *definitive*

---

[79] Herman Ridderbos, *The Coming of the Kingdom* (St. Catherines, Ontario: Paideia Press, 119621 1978), pp. 62ff.

(as distinguished from the *progressive* and *consummative*)[80] binding of satan was played out in the destruction of the Old Covenant system. This is why Apostle Paul, writing a few years before the event, could assure the Church that *"the God of peace will soon crush satan under your feet"* (Romans 16:20).

satan is to remain bound, Apostle John tells us, for a thousand years-a large, rounded-off number. We have seen that, as the number *seven* connotes a fullness of *quality* in Biblical imagery, the number *ten* contains the idea of a fullness of *quantity;* in other words, it stands for *'manyness'.* A thousand multiplies and intensifies this (10 x 10 x 10), in order to express great vastness (cf. 5:11; 7:4-8; 9:16; 11:3, 13; 12:6; 14:1,3,20). An analogy of this Scriptural usage is the way we, with a more inflationary mentality, use the term *million:* "I've told you a million times!" (I suspect that even "literalists" talk that way on occasion.)[81]

The last battle of the Revelation: Revelation 20:7-10

And when the thousand years are ended, slatan will be loosed from his prison and will come out to deceive the nations which are at the four corners of the earth, that is, Gog and Magog, to gather them for battle; their number is like the sand of the sea. And they marched up over the broad earth and surrounded the camp of the saints and the beloved city; but fire came down from heaven and consumed them, and the devil who had deceived them was thrown into the lake of fire and sulphur where the beast and the false prophet were, and they will be tormented day and night for ever and ever.

Russell makes a very strong point which I am in agreement with. The rest of the Book of Revelation is a visionary experience, yet in this passage, John is not seeing a vision but begins to declare a prophecy. He has moved from operating as a seer with a vision to interpret, and he has started

---

[80] satan is bound *progressively* as Christ's Kingdom grows throughout history, extending its influence to transform every aspect of life (Matt. 5:13-16; 13:31-33), and in the daily experience of Christians as we successfully resist the devil (James 4:7) and proclaim the Word of God (Rev. 12:10. satan will be bound *consummatively* at the Last Day, when death itself is destroyed in the Resurrection (John 6:39-40; 1 Cor. 15:22-26, 51-54). On the definitive-progressive- final pattern in general, see David Chilton, *Paradise Restored: A Biblical Theology of Dominion* (Ft. Worth, TX: Dominion Press, 1985), pp. 24f., 42, 73, 136, 146ff., 206, 209, 223.

[81] Quoted in David Chilton, Days of Vengeance (Dallas, GA: Dominion Press, 1987), 507.

operating as a Prophet speaking declaratively regarding the future. This act of seizing, chaining, and casting into the abyss is represented as taking place under the eye of the Seer, being introduced by the usual formula, *"And I saw."* It is an act of contemporaneous, or nearly so, with the judgments executed on the other criminals, the harlot and the beast. This part of the vision, then, falls within the proper limits of apocalyptic vision....[82]

To say it another way, ninety-nine percent of Revelation is a vision with symbols to interpret regarding the destruction of the Old Covenant world and the establishment of the New Covenant. Yet there is one percent of the Book of Revelation, found in chapter 20, that passes outside the time and space restrictions of the rest of the book and speaks of the distant future. This is clearly shown by the figurative use of the idiom, one thousand years.

Most scholars believe several parts of Revelation 20 speak to future events that have not yet been fulfilled. While Revelation is the revealing and unveiling of Jesus Christ and His New Covenant—which removed the Old Covenant veil—the contents of Revelation 20:7–15 were not fulfilled in AD 70. This includes satan's release from prison and his final battle against the people of God, after which he is thrown into the lake of fire. It also includes the great white throne judgement. These two events will happen at the end of the millennium. We do not know how long from now this will be since the idiom one thousand indicates simply a really long time.

As the famous Bible scholar, Milton Terry, wrote:

> How long the King of kings will continue His battle against evil and defer the last decisive blow, when satan shall be "loosed for a little time," no man can even approximately judge. It may require a million years.[83]

We live within this unique time in history, the millennium, during which we are partnering with God in His progressive expansion of the Kingdom on earth. This is a truly exciting revelation.

Here in Revelation we see this prophetic projection concerning satan. It declares that satan would be loosed from the prison that Jesus assigned

---

[82] James Stuart Russell, The Parousia (Grand Rapids, MI: Baker Books, 1983), 514.
[83] Milton Terry, Biblical Apocalyptics (Whitefish, MT: Kessinger Publishing, 2009), 451.

him to, and he now has an assignment to wage a final war against the Saints and the Church of Jesus Christ, but he and his demonic hoards are beaten with a final blow from the Lord. They are then cast into the lake of fire and sulphur where they would be tormented day and night forever.

UNDERSTANDING GOD AND MAGOG

I was born again in 1979 and in my early years of walking with the Lord and His Church I heard this in so many places.

In 1970, Hal Lindsey wrote a book titled "The Late Great Planet Earth." This book turned out to be a best seller with approximately 35 million copies being sold. His writing deeply affected a generation of Pastors, young leaders, and many Saints growing up in the Lord during the early 1970s and beyond. The lasting fruit of this book has created a generation that believes more in Lindsey's mythology than understanding what the Bible and history actually teach. In his book, Hal Lindsey concluded that, since the United States was not mentioned in Daniel or Revelation, it would not be a major player on the world scene when the Great Tribulation happened.

Based on his interpretation of various biblical texts, he also presumed that the European Economic Community (now the European Union) would become what he termed the "United States of Europe." This union would have ten members and would become, according to Lindsey, the revived Roman Empire, ruled by the antichrist, needed to fulfill Bible prophecy. We all now know that his reasoning was wrong, as the European Union now has twenty-seven members.

Then in 1982 Hal Lindsey released another book titled "The 1980s: Countdown to Armageddon", implying that the battle of Armageddon would happen soon. He even went so far as to say, "The decade of the 1980s could very well be the last decade of history as we know it,"[84] and he suggested that the United States would be destroyed by a surprise Soviet attack. Not surprisingly, because of Lindsey's adamant insistence that the 1980s would usher in the Great Tribulation, the book was quietly taken out of print in the early 1990s. Lindsey, however, would not give up. In the early 1990s, he published Planet Earth—2,000A.D., which warned Christians that they should not plan to still be living on earth by the year 2,000.

---

[84] Hal Lindsey The 1980s: Countdown to Armageddon (NYC, NY: Bantam Books, 1982), 8.

Throughout his several books, Lindsey assumed that the Cold War would continue until the end and, in fact, play a significant part in the unfolding of "end-time" events. He even went on to name Russia as the famous Gog of Revelation 20:8. Likewise, Lindsey believed the hippie culture of the 1960s and '70s would become the dominate culture in the United States, ultimately leading to the immorality and false religion "prophesied" to arise in the "end times" by various Bible passages. Clearly, none of these prophecies have come to pass, and many have been proven wrong due to the dates ascribed to them, yet Lindsey is still lauded by many Christians as a great modern Prophet.

Then in 1995, he began what turned out to be the mega-bestselling book series, "Left Behind". Due to the paranoia and fear regarding Y2K, Christians were primed for rapture fever. When all was said and done, Y2K was all hype, and 60 million copies of Left Behind had been sold (as well as three terrible feature length films that were similar in nature and theology to the Thief in the Night movie series of the 1970s).

Now we are in the new millennium, and it is high time that we begin to deeply question the modern "end time" views. If a teacher has been proclaiming that the end of the world is coming soon for over forty years, we should stop paying attention. If a teacher has proclaimed over forty different people to be the antichrist, we should ignore him. The fact that these teachers wear suits and are on TV doesn't make them any less wrong than the crazy guy on the street corner wearing a sandwich board sign that reads, "The end is near!" If a teacher was a paranoid alarmist regarding Y2K, we shouldn't be concerned about that teacher's other futuristic proclamations.

In my forty years of walking with the Lord and studying His Word, there have been numerous prophecies about the rapture, the "Second Coming" of Jesus and the end of the world, and they have all been proven wrong and false. And I would dare say that all those now being proclaimed and for those to be proclaimed in the future would all be false. I firmly believe this because when the Bible speaks about the end, it was never referring to the end of the world but to the end of the Old Covenant system and Jerusalem, which occurred in circa AD 70.

So, the teaching that Jesus' words in Matthew 24, the prophecies of Daniel, and the Book of Revelation are all referring to future events is a new concept, which came as a reaction to the Reformation. It has become deeply imbedded in the American evangelical community, but it does not have the support of Church history or Scripture.

In our next chapter we will begin exploring the new Heavens and the new Earth, and the New Temple in the earth.

CHAPTER TWELVE
THE NEW HEAVENS AND NEW EARTH

AS WE BEGIN THIS CHAPTER, I WOULD LIKE TO REMIND YOU OF THIS STATEMENT from James Russell, which was quoted earlier: he makes a very strong point in his book The Parousia, which I agree with. And I quote:

The rest of the Book of Revelation is a visionary experience, yet in this passage, John is not seeing a vision but begins to declare a prophecy. He has moved from operating as a seer with a vision to interpret, and he has started operating as a Prophet speaking declaratively regarding the future.

This act of seizing, chaining, and casting into the abyss is represented as taking place under the eye of the Seer, being introduced by the usual formula, *"And I saw."* It is an act of contemporaneous, or nearly so, with the judgments executed on the other criminals, the harlot and the beast. This part of the vision, then, falls within the proper limits of apocalyptic vision....

To say it another way, ninety-nine percent of Revelation is a vision with symbols to interpret regarding the destruction of the Old Covenant world and the establishment of the New Covenant.

Yet there is one percent of the Book of Revelation, found in chapter 20, that passes outside the time and space restrictions of the rest of the book and speaks of the distant future. This is clearly shown by the figurative use of the idiom, one thousand years.

Most scholars believe several parts of Revelation 20 speak to future events that **have not yet been fulfilled**. While Revelation is the revealing and unveiling of Jesus Christ and His New Covenant—which removed the Old Covenant veil—*the contents of Revelation 20:7-15 were not fulfilled in AD 70. This includes satan's release from prison and his final battle against the people of God, after which he is thrown into the lake of fire. It also includes the great white throne judgement. These two events will happen at the end of the millennium.* We do not know how long from now this will be since the idiom one thousand indicates simply a really long time. So let us now move on with this chapter:

We continue by dealing with a source of controversy that has been debated for many decades. And it is this: Revelation 20:1-3

Then I saw an angel coming down from heaven, holding in his hand the key of the bottomless pit and a great chain. And he seized the dragon, that ancient serpent, who is the devil and satan, and bound him for a thousand years, and threw him into the pit, and shut it and sealed it over him, that he should deceive the nations no more, till the thousand years were ended. After that he must be loosed for a little while.

This passage has been the source of much speculation. It has been the source of countless debates, divisions, novels, and poor-quality Christian movies.

People have attempted all sorts of wild interpretations of this passage, but I believe the true meaning is much simpler and more straightforward.

To begin, we must remind ourselves that Revelation is rife with symbolism. This is essential to understanding the so-called millennium (which just means one thousand years). Nowhere else in Scripture is a thousand-year time period specifically mentioned. In fact, to the Jewish people, the number one thousand simply meant "a whole lot." Again, remember we are talking about a letter being written to Saints living in the First Century, and not in the 21st Century...

Ok, so let us look at a few examples of how First Century thought by looking at a few passages of Scripture:

I agree with what Jonathan Welton have to say about this in his book "The Art of Revelation" as follows:

People have attempted all sorts of wild interpretations of this passage, but I believe the true meaning is much simpler and more straightforward. To begin, we must remind ourselves that Revelation is rife with symbolism. This is essential to understanding the so-called millennium (which just means one thousand years). Nowhere else in Scripture is a thousand-year time period specifically mentioned. In fact, to the Jewish people, the number one thousand simply meant "a whole lot." For example, look at the song in First Samuel 18, "Saul has slain his thousands, and David his tens of thousands" (1 Samuel 18:7). This sounds impressive, except that David had only killed Goliath. The Jewish approach to numbers was not the same as the modern literalism we have been taught.

Another example is the claim that God owns the cattle on a thousand hills in Psalm 50:10. Actually, God owns all the cattle on all the hills of the planet, yet to the Jewish reader, using the number one thousand was not limiting God's cattle ownership! A third example is in this verse: "Better is one day in your courts than a thousand elsewhere..." (Psalm 84:10). If understood literally, this verse would mean 1,001 days elsewhere would be better than a day in the house of God. Clearly, that was not the psalmist's message. The point is, based on this precedent, the number one thousand used in Revelation 20 does not refer to a literal one thousand years but to a long period of time.[85]

The Apostle John then goes on to explain to us what would occur during the one thousand years or the millennium reign: Revelation 20:4

Then I saw thrones, and seated on them were those to whom judgment was committed. Also I saw the souls of those who had been beheaded for their testimony to Jesus and for the word of God, and who had not worshiped the beast or its image and had not received its mark on their foreheads or their hands. They came to life, and reigned with Christ a thousand years.

Once again, I agree with what Jonathan Welton share in his book, "The Art of Revelation", where he said the following:

---
[85] Welton, Jonathan. The Art of Revelation. BookBaby. Kindle Edition.

The English translation of this passage makes it seem like there are two groups of people in view here, yet in the Greek it is clear that John was describing one group of people, the same group from Revelation 6:9–11:

When he opened the fifth seal, I saw under the altar the souls of those who had been slain because of the word of God and the testimony they had maintained. They called out in a loud voice, "How long, Sovereign Lord, holy and true, until you judge the inhabitants of the earth and avenge our blood?" Then each of them was given a white robe, and they were told to wait a little longer, until the full number of their fellow servants, their brothers and sisters, were killed just as they had been."

In chapter 6, we find these martyrs under the throne crying out for justice, but in chapter 20, the same martyrs are given thrones of their own to reign upon! We know this because of the next verse, which says, *"(The rest of the dead did not come to life until the thousand years were ended.) This is the first resurrection"* (Revelation 20:5).

This phrase, *"The rest of the dead,"* makes it clear that this group of people is a select number from among the dead. To find out what separates these ones who reign on thrones from "the rest," we need to look at the passage right before chapter 20 begins:

But the beast was captured, and with it the false prophet who had performed the signs on its behalf. With these signs he had deluded those who had received the mark of the beast and worshiped its image. The two of them were thrown alive into the fiery lake of burning sulfur. The rest were killed with the sword coming out of the mouth of the rider on the horse, and all the birds gorged themselves on their flesh (Revelation 19:19–21).

The ones in question, *"The rest of the dead,"* were those who died in the AD 70 destruction, the non-believing Jews. We know this to be true because the time indicator in Revelation 19:20 tells us this happened at the same time as the destruction of the beast and the false prophet, that is Nero and the Jewish rulers. Here is what we find in Revelation 20:

- A time period that is very long, symbolized by the number one thousand
- First Century martyrs sitting on thrones and passing judgment
- First Century Jewish non-believers being judged
- The dragon (devil) being bound in his ability to deceive the nations
- Importantly, we have not found any of the following popular ideas:
- A rebuilt Temple in Jerusalem
- The reestablishment of the Old Covenant system
- Jesus reigning physically upon the earth

These concepts that are not found in Revelation 20 have been injected when teachers take passages from Jeremiah, Zechariah, Ezekiel, and Isaiah and take them out of context to make them fit with Revelation 20.

If I were to simply paraphrase my understanding of Revelation 20, I would explain it this way: The thousand years represents the Kingdom of God. When Jesus came to earth, He bound the devil (the strong man, as in Matthew 12:28–29), and the devil could no longer deceive the nations (see Revelation 20:3). This paved the way for the disciples to disciple all nations (see Matthew 28:18–20). The First Century martyrs were given thrones to reign upon in the Kingdom; this occurred in Revelation 11, when Jesus was declared the King over the kingdoms of the earth (see Revelation 11:15) and the first resurrection was indicated (see Revelation 11:17–18). We now live inside the Kingdom of God on the earth, which is growing as the mustard seed and as the leaven going through the loaf (see Matthew 13:31–33). We are in the millennial reign, which is a spiritual Kingdom that is bringing Heaven into the earth progressively (see Matthew 6:10). Someday in the future, the Kingdom will have advanced so far that the only thing remaining to do will be to judge the devil finally and completely. He will be released from his chains to gather up whoever still resists the Kingdom, and the lot of them will be thrown into the lake of fire.[86]

I would like to further add this to what Jonathan Welton has said pertaining to Revelation 20 and the binding and losing of satan after a long period of time [one thousand years]. I believe that binding was accomplished when Jesus came in judgement upon Jerusalem and the Temple in circa AD 70, which was spoken consistently about during Jesus'

---

[86] Ibid.

prophecy recorded in Matthew 24, and in many other places throughout the New Testament.

At that time when He came in judgement; satan was bound and cast into the pit for a very long time [represented by the one thousand years], at which time the Church of Jesus Christ was established and grew [*because as we read about the days of the early Church we do not see the level of demonic activity as occurred when Jesus walked the face of the earth*] and grew and the Kingdom of God that came with Jesus expanded and continues to expand across the nations of the earth, Jesus is prophesied here in Revelation 20 to once again physically come to earth and this time to perform what is considered to be the final judgement after the devil is loosed for a short season. When he would gather his demons and those who refused to submit to God's Kingdom rule in the earth to make one final attack against the Church, but they would be utterly defeated and bound and cast into the lake of fire forever.

At this time human history will come to an end. And as I said before I do not believe that this earth would ever end. However, I do believe that the Kingdom of God would take over the earth and secure it for God to come and rule from here. Heaven will be on earth, and we would be restored to what Father had originally planned when He created Adam and Eve in the Garden of Eden at the launch of human history.

Remember that Daniel was able to interpret King Nebuchadnezzar's dream (see Daniel 2) where he interpreted that the Kingdom of God would come into the earth as small stone cut out of the Mountain of God and destroy the Roman Empire and that it would grow and grow until, it filled the entire earth. Hence the reason for me believing that God is going to set up His Headquarters in the earth!

In the last two chapters of Revelation, we find what many people have understood as a description of Heaven. This is what I grew up believing. I thought Revelation 21–22 described the time after the final judgment. Since then I have realized that these chapters actually describe life within the New Covenant.

To understand this, we must first understand some of the terms used in these chapters, particularly the new heavens and new earth. These are said to descend out of Heaven: "coming down out of heaven from God" (Revelation 21:2, 10). From this, we can gather that there are two heavens, the Heaven where God lives on His throne and the new heaven that descends to the earth. This is clarified further when we see two opposing thoughts about the Temple. The new heaven, which descends to the earth, has no Temple: "I did not see a temple in the city, because the Lord God Almighty and the Lamb are its Temple" (Revelation 21:22). Yet, the Heaven where God is enthroned does have a Temple:

Then God's temple in heaven was opened, and within his temple was seen the ark of his covenant. And there came flashes of lightning, rumblings, peals of thunder, an earthquake and a severe hailstorm (Revelation 11:19; see also Hebrews 9:23–24).

From this, it seems clear that the Book of Revelation speaks about two different heavens, with the Heaven where God dwells being the place of the afterlife. So, we must ask ourselves, how did the First Century reader understand the new heaven and new earth? Was it a figure of speech, or does it speak of literal places? To answer this, we need to start with the basic understanding of "heaven and earth" in the First Century.

In Matthew 5:18, Jesus says:

For truly I tell you, until heaven and earth disappear, not the smallest letter, not the least stroke of a pen, will by any means disappear from the Law until everything is accomplished.

Many of us have read this many times without thinking through the implications of this verse. It gives us a choice between two options. Either Heaven and earth still exist, and we are under 100 percent of the Old Covenant Law, or Heaven and earth have disappeared, along with the Law. If we understand Heaven and earth to be the literal physical earth and heavens (sky), then we must believe that 100 percent of the Mosaic Old Covenant Law is still in force until the end of this planet. This includes the Temple sacrifices, the three annual pilgrimages to Jerusalem, and many other rules that none of us follow. After all, Jesus said, "*...not the smallest letter, not the least stroke of a pen, will by any means disappear from the Law...*"

Obviously, this does not sit right with most of us, because it violates what we understand about the transition from the Old Covenant to the New. Alternatively, Jesus could have been using a figure of speech that everyone in the First Century understood. This is the only other option for how we can understand this verse. Either Jesus was talking about something else, or the Law is currently 100 percent in effect until the planet is destroyed.

We gain another clue about this puzzle in Jesus' mention of Heaven and earth in Matthew 24:35, where He says, *"Heaven and earth will pass away, but My words will not pass away."* Matthew 24 is about the destruction of the Temple in the First Century. So, why did Jesus throw in and add this statement here? The answer would have been obvious to First Century readers, but not so obvious to us. Jews in the First Century referred to the Temple system as Heaven and earth.

Sources as early as Josephus suggest that the very design of the Temple was modeled after the design of heaven and earth:

> . . .for if any one do but consider the fabric of the tabernacle, and take a view of the garments of the high priest, and of those vessels which we make use of in our sacred ministration, he will find that our legislator was a divine man, and that we are unjustly reproached by others; for if any one do without prejudice, and with judgment, look upon these things, he will find they were everyone made in way of imitation and representation of the universe. When Moses distinguished the tabernacle into three parts, and allowed two of them to the priests, as a place accessible and common, he denoted the land and the seas, these being of general access to all; but he set apart the third division for God, because heaven is inaccessible to men.[87]

From this, we can gather that heaven and earth was a metaphor for the Temple system. According to John Lightfoot, the highly respected author of A Commentary on the New Testament from the Talmud and Hebraica, the *"passing away of heaven and earth"* is the "destruction of Jerusalem and the whole Jewish state...as if the whole frame of this world were to be dissolved."[88]

Maimonides, writing in the 12th Century, also confirmed this view of the phrase heaven and earth, saying:

---

[87] Josephus, Antiquities of the Jews, Book 3, Chapter 7.
[88] Was quoted in Gary DeMar, Last Days Madness, 4th ed. (Atlanta, GA: American Vision, 1999), 192.

The Arabs likewise [as the Hebrew Prophets] say of a person who has met with a serious accident, "His heavens, together with his earth, have been covered"; and when they speak of the approach of a nation's prosperity, they say, "The light of the sun and moon has increased," A new heaven and a new earth has been created," or they use similar phrases.[89]

If we use this idea to interpret Jesus' words in Matthew 5:18, it suddenly begins to make a lot of sense. Jesus wasn't saying that the Law would hold true until the physical earth was destroyed, but until the metaphorical heaven and earth, or the Old Covenant Temple system was destroyed. It makes sense that when the Old Covenant ended, the Temple would need to be destroyed along with it, and that is exactly what happened in AD 70. This may seem like a huge shift in thinking, but when we make that shift, we can see that it actually relieves a burden that many Christians have unnecessarily lived under simply because they did not understand the metaphor Jesus used. Charles Spurgeon sums it up well when he says:

> Did you ever regret the absence of the burnt-offering, or the red heifer, or any one of the sacrifices and rites of the Jews? Did you ever pine for the feast of tabernacles, or the dedication? No, because, though these were like the old heavens and earth to the Jewish Believers, they have passed away, and we now live under new heavens and a new earth, so far as the dispensation of the divine teaching is concerned. The substance is come, and the shadow has gone, and we do not remember it.[90]

In the next chapter we would be exploring the end of the Revelation and what it reveals to us.

---

[89] Maimonides, The Guide for the Perplexed, 204.
[90] Charles H. Spurgeon, Metropolitan Tabernacle Pulpit, Vol. 37 (Banner of Truth Publications, 1970), 354.

CHAPTER THIRTEEN
Closing the Revelation

AS WAS MENTIONED PREVIOUSLY, THE INTRODUCTION AND THE EPILOGUE ARE a beautiful frame to the content of the Book of Revelation. As with the introduction, let's look briefly at the text of the closing of this book to see how it contextualizes the rest of the book.

> Look, I am coming soon! My reward is with me, and I will give to each person according to what they have done. I am the Alpha and the Omega, the First and the Last, the Beginning and the End (Revelation 22:12-13).

When Napoleon Bonaparte wrote that he would attack soon, he didn't mean in our future. When Abraham Lincoln wrote of ending slavery soon, he wasn't referring to our future. So why would we think Jesus was talking about our future when He said soon? Only by doing violence and disrespect to the text can we reinterpret soon to mean not soon. The destruction of Jerusalem was soon for the original readers of Revelation, and Jesus was exactly right in declaring it was soon.

> Blessed are those who wash their robes, that they may have the right to the tree of life and may go through the gates into the city. Outside are the dogs, those who practice magic arts, the sexually

immoral, the murderers, the idolaters and everyone who loves and practices falsehood (Revelation 22:14-15).

In the First Century, individuals had two Jerusalems to pick from. If they accepted Jesus as their Lord and Messiah, they spiritually went through the gates and entered into the heavenly Jerusalem, that is, the Bride of Christ, the Church. In contrast, if they chose to not partake in the heavenly Jerusalem, they chose the earthly Jerusalem, which was filled with evil and about to be judged, by default.

I, Jesus, have sent my angel to give you this testimony for the churches. I am the Root and the Offspring of David, and the bright Morning Star (Revelation 22:16).

The churches on earth had been through nearly forty years of incredible persecution since Jesus had left, and it was time for an update from Heaven. As Jerusalem stood on the eve of incredible tragedy, Jesus gave an update to His followers on earth.

The Spirit and the bride say, "Come!" And let the one who hears say, "Come!" Let the one who is thirsty come; and let the one who wishes take the free gift of the water of life. I warn everyone who hears the words of the prophecy of this scroll: If anyone adds anything to them, God will add to that person the plagues described in this scroll. And if anyone takes words away from this scroll of prophecy, God will take away from that person any share in the tree of life and in the Holy City, which are described in this scroll. He who testifies to these things says, "Yes, I am coming soon." Amen. Come, Lord Jesus. The grace of the Lord Jesus be with God's people. Amen (Revelation 22:17-21).

Verses 18 and 19 are quite interesting and have been many times quoted through the ages. My simple thought is this: If people in the First Century changed the context and content of this prophecy regarding the impending destruction of Jerusalem (see verse 20), others could easily misinterpret and misunderstand the text. That would result in Christians being trapped inside Jerusalem during the destruction. It was absolutely imperative for the whole content of Revelation to remain intact simply because it was Jesus' directions to the churches in the First Century for how to avoid the destruction.

As we know from Raptureless, every single Christian in the First Century understood the Olivet discourse and the Book of Revelation; thus, Albert Barnes records,

> "Not one Christian perished in the destruction of that city [Jerusalem]"[91]

Because they knew the passages were about their near future, they knew when to flee to the nearby mountains. The Book of Revelation was an invaluable blessing in the First Century, but as time passed and the events of the First Century and AD 70 faded into the distant past, people ceased to understand Revelation's purpose for those living right before the AD 70 destruction. This is the correct way to understand this seemingly mysterious book.[92]

[93]Dr. John Noe says it powerfully – What is its relevance for us today?

In the middle of the unfolding apocalyptic drama of the breaking of the seals, the sounding of the trumpets, and pouring out of the vials, is a drastic instruction given to John that is downplayed by most commentators. In Revelation chapter ten, the angel of the Lord instructs John to *eat the scroll* (Revelation 10:9b). This is the same sealed scroll handed to the Lamb for Him to open in Revelation chapter five. Why was John told to perform such a graphic and grotesque act? (Have you eaten any good books lately?)

Let's not forget that this instruction is contained in a book filled with signs and symbols. The reason is, as we shall further see, God did not intend the prophetic message in this scroll (the book of Revelation) to be limited to one particular time period and one particular people—i.e., for John's original audience, the seven churches and the Christians of that 1st Century alone. Fact is, the physical act of eating and ingesting something always transforms it. And so, the whole of the prophecy of the book of Revelation is transformed.

---

[91] Albert Barnes, Barnes' Notes on the New Testament (1832), Matthew 24.
[92] Welton, Jonathan. Raptureless: An Optimistic Guide to the End of the World - Revised Edition Including The Art of Revelation. BookBaby. Kindle Edition.
[93] Researched at, https://www.prophecyrefi.org/our-teachings/book-of-revelation/what-is-its-relevance-for-us-today/

Immediately after John ate the scroll, he was commanded to regurgitate it, if you will; but this time it is directed to a different audience. The angel told him, *"You must prophesy again about many peoples, nations, languages, and kings"* (Revelation 10:11). When you couple this statement with the angel's later instructions to John, *"do not seal up the words of the prophecy of this book, because the time is at hand"* (Revelation 22:10), it should soon become clear that the Revelation's prophecy was not exhausted in its A.D. 70 fulfillment. Its relevance was broadened from its primary fulfillment audience and focus to a different audience and focus.

Below are six additional insights supporting a universal application and timeless relevance of this prophecy beyond its A.D. 70 fulfillment. This is what theologians call a *sensus plenior*—i.e. "a fuller sense . . . the possibility of more significance to . . . [a] passage than was consciously apparent to the original author...." (Virkler, *Hermeneutics*, 25).

Again, and *first and foremost*, the *whole* of this prophecy, from first to last, was written to encourage its original audience. They were under severe persecution and in need of relief. This is the Revelation's primary focus. The *whole* of it, therefore, is rooted, time-restricted, and fulfilled in one, immediate, specific, and real coming of Jesus Christ in judgment in A.D. 70. That contemporary and historical setting was Revelation's one and only fulfillment. And this historical fulfillment must play a controlling role as we explore a *sensus plenior*.

Secondly, John's prophesying "again about many peoples, nations, languages and kings" (Revelation 10:9-11), is clearly a different and broader group of recipients of this prophecy than John's original area and audience of the seven churches (Revelation 1:4, 11). Traditionally, however, commentators have tried to minimize the meaning of this dramatic symbolism of John's eating the scroll and prophesying again. They contend it only meant a personal application for John. Suggested applications (in *italics*), along with our comments, include:

- *John must yet receive the rest of the prophecy (chapters 11-22)*. But John was not going anywhere. He was there for the duration. This explanation is not only highly reductionistic, in comparison with the dramatic symbolism used, it is superfluous and weak.
- *John would later travel throughout the area of the seven churches sharing this prophecy verbally (a book tour of sorts)*. But it was not

necessary for John to travel about doing this. That was the purpose of sending the letters. They were to be read aloud in the seven churches.
- *This was a commissioning for John.* But John had already been commissioned on at least two previous occasions (see Revelation 1:10-20 and 4:1-2), and also in Revelation 1:19. Therefore, another commissioning would be unnecessary and overly redundant.

Thirdly, similar expressions are found five other times in Revelation 5:9; 7:9; 13:7; 14:6; and 17:15 (also see Revelation 22:9 and Daniel 4:1; 7:14). In Revelation 5:9, for example, this expression universalizes the application of Jesus' sacrifice: "And they sang a new song; 'You [Jesus] are worthy to take the scroll and to open its seals, because you were slain, and with your blood you purchased men [and women] for God from every tribe and language and people and nation." That includes us, and hopefully you as well.

Fourthly, if this expression's use in Revelation 10:11 is consistent with this book's other five uses, and we employ the interpretative principle of letting "Scripture interpret Scripture," then it must carry the same universalized and timeless meaning here. This widening of application is the textual rationale for applying the *whole* prophecy beyond its A.D. 70 fulfillment. Hence, the words of this climactic prophecy refer and pertain to all peoples and nations throughout the world. We must also specially note that in Revelation 10:11, "kings" replaced "'tribes' as the fourth element in the quartet. In Revelation 1:6 and 5:10, believers are called "kings." Thus, the Apocalypse is concerned with the whole of humankind from both a corporate and an individual sense. This universal and timeless application, beyond its fulfillment, is the most natural way to understand a consistent use of this terminology.

Fifthly, the Revelation's fulfillment (its realities, blessings, judgments, principles, and portrayals, which cannot be limited to a one-time, historic, and static eschatological fulfillment for its own day, which it was, or to someday still out in the future) serves in a typological and controlling manner. Thus, the fulfillment of Revelation's imagery and visions now serves as a type for repeating patterns of Christ's ongoing involvement and activity in history and in individual lives. In other words, John's prophecy now transcends its fulfillment time and context into new historical and personal applications, globally. Post A.D. 70, this prophecy is not only timeless but also multifaceted.

This ongoing relevancy and timelessness, universal applications are part of the Revelation's uniqueness and further differentiate it from Jesus' Olivet Discourse in Matthew 24, Mark 13, and Luke 21, which cover the same fulfillment time frame and events. However, the Revelation's ongoing aspects resist predictability because John's prophesying "again" was general and not time-sensitive or place-specific. The whole book echoes this relevancy theme that it is for all who live and die for Christ from that time on (Revelation 14:12-13).

Hence, the Revelation is still an open book and meant to be forever kept open from the time of its writing forward. Its exciting message proclaims the ongoing involvement of Jesus Christ in the struggles of the spirit realm and the physical/material realm, for all ages. Such a reformed application can help us better understand the rise and fall of empires, the history of nations, the lives of people, the comings and goings of groups, institutions, and other corporate bodies. They, indeed, are controlled by God and Christ (also see Daniel 2:21). Moreover, this textual understanding of Revelation's ongoing relevance and timeless applications secures its meaningfulness from the time of its fulfillment onward for all periods of Church and world history.

The Revelation also warns, *"If anyone adds anything to them, God will add to him the plagues described in this book. And if anyone takes away from this book of prophecy, God will take away from him his share in the tree of life and in the holy city, which are described in this book"* (Revelation 22:18-19). Let us urge you to constantly make sure that no message you believe, or present adds to or takes away from the content and the spirit of the Apocalypse. These two dire warnings and consequences are just as relevant for us today as they were for the Revelation's original audience. If not, they are toothless. In our opinion, any modern-day interpretation that relegates the relevance of all or any portion of this prophecy solely to the past or solely to the future is at risk of violating these warnings and opening oneself to their consequences.

This ongoing relevancy also perfectly corresponds with God's redemptive grace and purpose. While totally local in fulfillment, all are universal in goal, scope, and application. Seen in this manner, the Revelation is truly a prophecy of *"the eternal gospel to proclaim to those who live on the earth – to every nation, tribe, language and people"* (Revelation 14:6).

Sixthly, there is no suggestion of a termination of these applications. The popular terminology of a "final" or "last judgment," a "final blessing," a "final coming," a "final day of the Lord," or a "final antichrist" is non-scriptural and unscriptural. Therefore, in the prophecy of the book of Revelation, we moderns have real, ongoing blessings, warnings, comings, judgments, and interactions of Christ with which to be personally involved and concerned (Revelation 1:3; 22:7, 14-19). Yet there is no "antichrist" contained therein. That notion has been imported into this book. Rather, "many antichrists," who fit the descriptions found *only* in 1 John 2:18, 22; 4:3; 2 John 7, still roam the earth today, as they did in the past and will continue in the future.

Make no mistake! This realization of the Revelation's ongoing relevancy is not a lesser reality or a second-rate option in comparison with solely past or mostly futuristic fulfillment views. In effect, it is more significant than any single view. Through the Revelation, God is equipping Believers of all generations with an understanding of how the world of the spirit operates and this revelation is the highest form of knowledge and wisdom revealed to humankind and is just as pertinent today as it was in the past and will be in the future.

It is the knowledge of how the Kingdom of God functions and how we can enter in effectively and victoriously, and live in it in this present world. Thus, nowadays, the entire vision of the Revelation is past, present, and future. It is the timeless unveiling of Jesus Christ as He is now, and not a timetable of yet-future events. To see this is to understand the Revelation as it was intended and to receive one of its blessings; not to see this is to miss its richest meaning, for in this greater Jesus Christ *"are hidden all the treasures of wisdom and knowledge"* (Colossians 2:3).

Our recognition of *both* the total fulfillment and total relevancy of *"the revelation of Jesus Christ"* (Revelation 1:1) in our lives, here and now, should create a greater sense of responsibility, a greater motivation for obedience, and a greater desire to worship than the traditional deferment views—past or future. God through Christ continues to act in history and in the lives of his saints in an apocalyptically revealed manner. [End of reference].

The book of Revelation is full of imagery that had specific meaning to the First Century Church and does not hold the same meaning to us in the 21st Century. Hence the reason we must study this book in its divinely inspired First Century context. Without that understanding we would read into this book that which is not there or even intended. This brings us to the end of our study. It is my earnest prayer that you would have benefited positively from this study. Now let me recommend some books for further reading and study. Some of which I have found to be very helpful in my ongoing study of the Word of God. And of course, you should eat the meat and throw away the bones.

- *The Greater Jesus* by Dr. John Noe
- *Unravelling the End* by Dr. John Noe
- *The Perfect Ending for the World* by Dr. John Noe
- *The Great Tribulation* by David Chilton
- *Days of Vengeance* by David Chilton (700-page masterpiece)
- *Raptureless: An Optimistic Guide to the End of the World* by Jonathan Welton
- *The Art of Revelation* by Jonathan Welton
- *The Beast of Revelation Identified* by Kenneth Gentry
- *Revelation for Everyone* by N. T. Wright
- *The Last Days According to Jesus* by R.C. Sproul
- *Last Days Madness* by Gary DeMar
- *Is Jesus Coming Soon?* by Gary DeMar
- *Victorious Eschatology* by Harold Eberle and Martin Trench
- *The Great Tribulation* by David Chilton
- *The Olivet Discourse Made Easy* by Kenneth Gentry
- *Whose Right It Is* by Kelley Varner
- *Exploding the Israel Deception* by Steve Wohlberg (Jewish Christian author)
- *Israel and Bible Prophecy* by John L. Bray
- *One Chapter in Last Days Madness* by Gary DeMar
- *Before Jerusalem Fell* by Kenneth Gentry
- *The Early Church and the End of the World* by Gary DeMar and Francis Gumerlock
- *Josephus: The Complete Works* by Flavius Josephus
- *The Early Church Understanding of the Endtimes* by Gary DeMar

- *The Early Church and the End of the World* by Gary DeMar
- *The Antichrist the Man of Sin of 2 Thessalonians 2* by John L. Bray
- *The Book of Revelation Made Easy* by Kenneth Gentry
- *Navigating the Book of Revelation* by Kenneth Gentry

OTHER EXCITING TITLES
By Michael Scantlebury

ARE WE LIVING IN THE END TIMES OR THE LAST DAYS?

Whenever we hear this term "end-times or last-days" it conjures up all kinds of images in our minds: from the universe blowing up with the largest flames you could ever imagine! And that it would usher in a new heaven and a new earth. We also have presupposed in the body of Christ that before all of this would indeed occur, the righteous would be raptured away and then the world would be left a massive fire of destruction.

When you hear Christians mention the 'last days,' many just assume it's referring to the end of time and of the world. But the attentive Bible student asks, 'last days of what?' It seems obvious to me that the text is referring to the end of the Old Covenant-Temple aeon/age. When you read the New Testament through these lenses, all I can say is WOW! It makes a significant difference, when you read the Scriptures with the realization that the Bible was written FOR you and not TO you.

We need to also understand that "time of the end" and "end of time" are not one and the same thing. The Bible teaches about the "time of the end" but there is nothing taught about an "end of time."

FATHERS AND SONS – AN UNVEILING

As we embark upon this study, there is something that I would like for us to first understand, and it is this: God the Father is the ultimate Father. There has never been anyone like Him, nor is there currently anyone like Him, nor will there ever be anyone like Him. He is in a class all by Himself.

Another thing that we need to understand moving forward is this: Respect produced by force and domination is not respect but fear.

Also, when we speak of sons, we are not only referring to the male gender, but we are speaking of **a new class in God**. Those that have been washed by the Blood of Jesus and have entered the New Covenant with Him. Notice that in the Scriptures, it never states "Sons and Daughters of God."

John 1:12 states

But as many as received him, he gave them power to be made the sons of God, to them that believe in his name. ...

As such, I do believe that women can also be Apostles and in a broader scope, they qualify to "father" should that mantle be upon them.

HEAVEN & EARTH A BIBLICAL UNDERSTANDING

Whenever we today in this 21st Century read about heaven and earth in the Scriptures we need to be careful as to exactly what is being referred to. And here are some reasons as to why this must be.

1. The original Bible was not written in our modern English, which is a far different language than Hebrew and Greek the original languages of the Holy Scriptures. Hence the reason for us to become avid students of the Word of God.

2. We, living today are not the original recipients of Scripture and as such we need to understand what the original recipients understood when they first received that Word.
3. We must be willing to let the Bible interpret itself and not hang on to our theories for the Scriptures.
4. That the Bible speaks of at least four Heavens and three earths. And as such we need to dig deep into the Word of God and find them and apply this understanding in our study.

Remember what the Scriptures say in Proverbs 25:2 *It is the glory of God to conceal the word, and the glory of kings to search out the speech.*

With that said let us now take a deeper dive and journey into the Word of God with the intention of extracting much needed revelation concerning these Heavens and Earths.

MY PONDERINGS

In this book before you the author has been engaged in pondering several subjects and as such, decided to put his thoughts in a book. As you read through these pages may the Lord use his thoughts to both inspire and bless you. Here are some of the subjects he has been pondering, with each one making up a chapter of this book:

My Ponderings on The Kingdom of God
My Ponderings on The Church
My Ponderings on Innovation
My Ponderings on Wisdom and The Power of Vision
My Ponderings on Navigating Seasons
My Ponderings on Breakthroughs
My Ponderings on Unity
My Ponderings on The Many Comings of Jesus
My Ponderings on Eschatology
My Ponderings on Jesus the First Fruit of the Dead
My Ponderings on Understanding the Times
My Ponderings on Understanding the New Covenant
My Ponderings on Gold

UNDERSTANDING THE KINGDOM OF GOD AND THE CHURCH OF JESUS CHRIST

"This book is a game changer and will teach you what it means to be part of This Kingdom."

Pastor Marilyn Bailey—Teleios Church, Johannesburg, South Africa

"There is perhaps no greater time to revisit the spiritual and practical understanding of the kingdom of God than right now.

Apostle Scantlebury addresses and corrects, common misconceptions, explains the contrasts in the Kingdom of God and the kingdom of darkness, properly aligns the Kingdom and the Church, and propels us toward a holistic understanding of Kingdom life in the earth.

With great patience and clear articulation, Apostle Scantlebury lays out a compelling case for the people of God to give priority to understanding and walking in the principles of the Kingdom of God in life and ministry.

Do yourself a favour; set aside some time to read through and study this transformative volume. You will be challenged, changed, and equipped to be a proper representative of the kingdom of God."

Apostle Eric L. Warren—Eric Warren Ministries Charlotte, North Carolina, USA

ESCHATOLOGY – A BIBLICAL VIEW

If you were a time traveler and traveled back to the time of say Abraham Lincoln and told him you were from the future in 21st century. What if he asked you how people communicated in the 21st century, and now you had to try and explain say how an email works. How would you explain it?

Would you use something he would be familiar with to describe it? Perhaps you would tell him that in the future postmen would ride horses at 500 mile per hour. Or you might tell

him you could deliver a message by train from New York to LA in less than one day. You're trying to find a way to communicate how "fast" an email really is. But you're trying to do in a way that wouldn't totally blow his mind.

That's kind of the conundrum we have when trying to understand difficult verses in the Bible, especially in themes like eschatology. The prophetic writers of Scripture had to convey God's mysteries in language that their readers would understand.

Fast forward now 2-3,000 years later, and we are reading these prophetic Scriptures through a 21st century lens, and sometimes coming up with all kinds of weird speculative interpretations because we didn't understand what those Scriptures would have meant to a first century Believer, or a Jew living in the time of the OT Prophets.

The book before you plan to delve deeper into this and much more as it seeks to present you with a sensible view of eschatology.

THE RESTORATION OF ZION

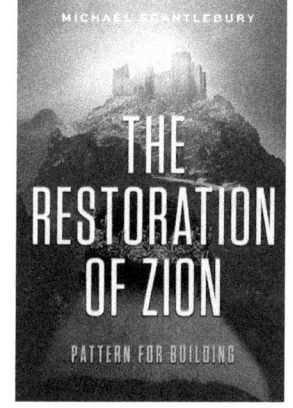

When you hear the word Zion, what comes to mind? As Christians, we've sung the choruses and the hymns about Zion or Mount Zion, but do we fully understand just what we're singing about? Do we know what it is? The Bible promises the full restoration of Zion, and if we don't fully know what Zion is, what then do we anticipate in terms of its restoration?

The greatest hindrance to accurate interpretation and application of Scripture is a futuristic view of Scripture. This futuristic view continues to rob the Believer of experiencing God in His fullness in the here and now.

In this book, we will uncover within the Scriptures exactly what Zion actually represents to the New Testament Believer. So lay down any preconceived ideas you may have, delve into the pages of this book, and let it speak truth to you.

AS IT WAS IN THE BEGINNING SO SHALL IT BE...

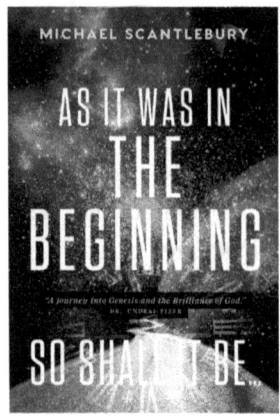

Have you ever wondered about life and all of its intricacies? Why are we here on planet earth? What is out there in deep dark space? Who created it all in its majesty and wonder with the brilliancy of everything that surrounds us?

Since time began, man has tried to explain things regarding the known world. One forward thinker put forth a theory that the world was flat. That was refuted by more research. Study and research and pondering some more have revealed some truth about our world but not all the questions are yet answered.

While many of us as Christians enjoy documentaries on the pondering of the many ways we may have "gotten here" beginning with the theory of alien transports dropping us off, to the idea of a cosmic slime pit which one day came to life, so truly the only authority we have as born-again followers of Jesus Christ is the book of Genesis, the very first book of the Holy Scriptures, which simply states: "In the beginning God created the heavens and the earth." Genesis 1:1

We will broach the answers to these and other questions only God's inspired word, the Holy Bible will answer the many questions at hand.

We will begin our journey into the heart and mind of this incredible Creator to learn the reason and purpose for our existence. And as we take that incredible journey, we would seek to come to terms with the revealed, eventual outcome of our existence and life upon planet earth.

STUDY GUIDE – DANIEL IN BABYLON

This is an exciting study into the present truth lifestyle illustrated through the lives of Daniel and his friends. Whether you'll be meeting with others in a group or going through this book on your own, you've made an excellent decision by choosing to read **DANIEL in Babylon** and studying it in-depth with this guide.

This is a seminal study with strong Apostolic messaging, yet its flowing style allows for easy assimilation of biblical truths, and provides accurate insights for the cerebral Believer, who like Daniel and his companions, are usually the target of the world system. In this book various methodologies are outlined through which, spiritual Babylon seeks to entice the brightest and best of every Godly generation, to acculturize, rob of spiritual identity and manipulate to promote world kingdom end.

PRINCIPLES FOR VICTORIOUS LIVING: VOL II

The initial purpose of the five-fold ministry is for the perfecting or maturing of the Saints, which leads to its next intention, which is the real work of the ministry of Jesus Christ, reconciling the world back to the Father. This book lends itself to help in the maturing of the Saints. It adds insight and strategies that help in achieving exponential personal growth preparing one for the real work of the ministry. This is a volume of information and revelation needed in such a time as this, when maturity and focus are the needed key components that bring us an overcoming victory in this realm and advance the Kingdom of God.

PRINCIPLES FOR VICTORIOUS LIVING: VOL I

The information contained herein is well balanced with a spiritual maturity that keenly stems from wisdom and revelation in the knowledge of Christ. This is the anointing of an Apostle, and the truths that our brother shares will certainly cause you to excel in the Kingdom of God long before this life is over when later we enter the eternals. There's so much to experience today in this life, and Michael extracts so much from the Word of God to facilitate that. His insight of revelation and ability to interpret and articulate what his spirit receives from the Lord are powerful.

PRESENT TRUTH LIFESTYLE – DANIEL IN BABYLON

This is a seminal study with strong Apostolic messaging, yet its flowing style allows for easy assimilation of biblical truths, and provides accurate insights for the cerebral Believer, who like Daniel and his companions, are usually the target of the world system. In this book various methodologies are outlined through which, spiritual Babylon seeks to entice the brightest and best of every Godly generation, to acculturize, rob of spiritual identity and manipulate to promote world kingdom end.

But thanks be to God, there is still a generation in the earth spiritually alert enough to operate within the world system, yet deploy their talents and giftings to bring honour and glory to God. Those with the Daniel mindset will decode dreams and visions and interpret judgements written on the kingdoms of this world in this season.

ESTHER PRESENT TRUTH CHURCH

In a season where the Church co-exists harmoniously with truth and error, this book provides us with a precision tool and well-calibrated instrument of change that is able to fine-tune the global Body of Christ.

The Book of Esther is rich with revelation that is still valid and applicable for the day in which we live. Hidden within its pages is a powerful "present truth" message. The lives of the people involved and the conditions that are seen have spiritual parallels for the Church. Our destiny as the Body of Christ is revealed. The preparations and conditions we must attain to are all similar.

THE FORTRESS CHURCH

According to Webster's English Dictionary "fortress" is defined as: a fortified place: stronghold, *especially*: A large and permanent fortification sometimes including a town. A place that is protected against attack. This book seeks to describe what is a "Fortress Church". We would be looking into the dynamics of this Church as described in Jacob's vision in Genesis Chapter 28, also as described by the Prophet Isaiah, in Isaiah Chapter 2 and as the one detailed in a Psalm of  the sons of Korah in Psalms Chapter 48. We would also be looking at a working model of this type of church as found at Antioch in the Book of Acts. Finally we would be exploring The Church at Ephesus, where the Apostle Paul by the Holy Spirit revealed some powerful descriptions of The Church.

CALLED TO BE AN APOSTLE

This autobiography spans fifty-two years of my life on the earth thus far and I have the hope of living several more... Our home was always packed with young people and we did enjoy times of really wonderful fellowship! Although we were experiencing these wonderful times of fellowship my appetite and desire to grow in the things of God continued unabated. I continued to read anything and everything that I could put my hands on that would strengthen my life. I began reading  Wigglesworth, Moody, Finney, Idahosa, Lake, and the list went on and on! But the more I read the more this question burned in my heart–"*why is it that every time we hear/read about a move of God, it is always miles away and in another country? Why can't I experience some of the things that I am reading about?*" Little did I know the Lord would answer that desire!

LEAVENED REVEALED

The Bible has a lot to say about *leaven* and its effects upon the Believer. Leaven as an ingredient gives a false sense of growth. In the New Testament there are at least six types of *leaven* spoken about and we will be exploring them in detail, in order to ensure that our lives are completely free of the first five, and completely influenced by the sixth! These types of leaven include the following: The leaven of the Pharisees; The leaven of the Sadducees; The leaven of the Galatians; The leaven of Herod; The leaven of the Corinthians. However, the Leaven of the Kingdom of God is the only type of leaven that has the power and capacity to bring about true growth and lasting change to our lives.

I WILL BUILD MY CHURCH — JESUS CHRIST

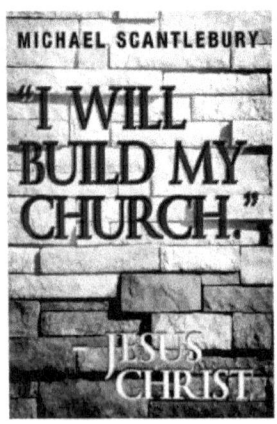

"For we are his *masterpiece*, created in Christ Jesus for good works that God prepared long ago to be our way of life." Ephesians 2:10

What a powerful picture of The Church of Jesus Christ–His Masterpiece! Reference to a *masterpiece* lends to the idea that there are other pieces and among them all, this particular one stands head and shoulders above the rest! This is so true when it comes to The Church that Jesus Christ is building; when you place it alongside everything else that God has created, The Church is by far His Masterpiece!

Other Exciting Titles

JESUS CHRIST THE APOSTLE AND HIGH PRIEST OF OUR PROFESSION

There is a dimension to the apostolic nature of Jesus Christ that I would like to capture in His one-on-one encounters with several people during the time He walked the face of the earth and functioned as Apostle. In this book we will explore several significant encounters that Jesus Christ had with different people where valuable principles and insight can be gleaned. They are designed to change your life.

FIVE PILLARS OF THE APOSTOLIC

It has become very evident that a new day has dawned in the earth, as the Lord restores the foundational ministry of the Apostle back to His Church. This book will give you a clear and concise understanding of what the Holy Spirit is doing in The Church today.

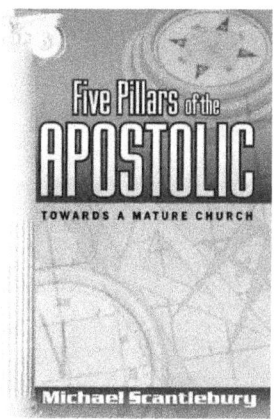

APOSTOLIC PURITY

In every dispensation, in every move of God's Holy Spirit to bring restoration and reformation to His Church, righteousness, holiness and purity has always been of utmost importance to the Lord. This book will challenge your to walk pure as you seek to fulfil God's Will for your life and ministry.

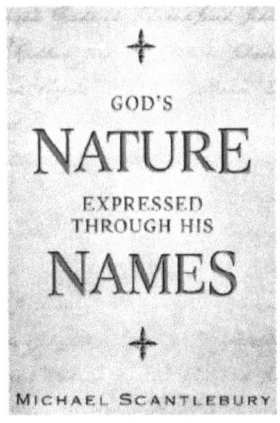

GOD'S NATURE EXPRESSED THROUGH HIS NAMES

How awesome it would be when we encounter God's Nature through the varied expressions of His Names. His Names give us reference and guidance as to how He works towards and in us as His people–and by extension to society! As a matter of fact it adds a whole new meaning to how you draw near to Him; and by this you can now begin to know His Ways because you have come into relationship with His Nature.

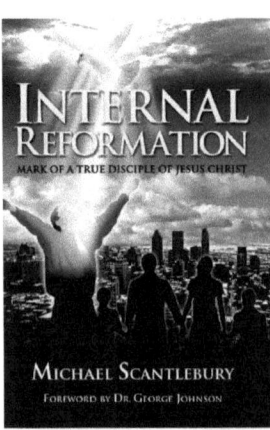

INTERNAL REFORMATION

Internal Reformation is multifaceted. It is an ecclesiology laying out the blue print of The Church Jesus Christ is building in today's world. At the same time it is a manual laying out the modus operandi of how Believers are called to function as dynamic, militant over-comers who are powerful because they carry internally the very character and DNA of Jesus Christ.

KINGDOM ADVANCING PRAYER VOL I

The Church of Jesus Christ is stronger and much more determined and equipped than she has ever been, and strong, aggressive, powerful, Spirit-Filled, Kingdom-centred prayers are being lifted in every nation in the earth. This kind of prayer is released from the heart of Father God into the hearts of His people, as we seek for His Glory to cover the earth as the waters cover the sea.

APOSTOLIC REFORMATION

If the axe is dull, And one does not sharpen the edge, Then he must use more strength; But wisdom brings success." (Ecclesiastes 10:10) For centuries The Church of Jesus Christ has been using quite a bit of strength while working with a dull axe (sword, Word of God, revelation), in trying to get the job done. This has been largely due to the fact that she has been functioning without Apostles, the ones who have been graced and anointed by the Lord, with the ability to sharpen.

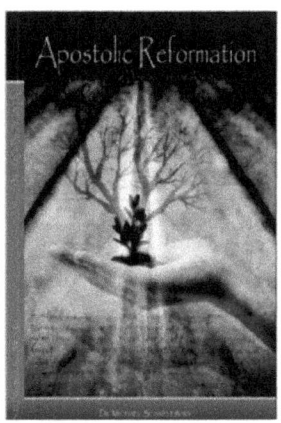

KINGDOM ADVANCING PRAYER VOL II

Prayer is calling for the Bridegroom's return, and for the Bride to be made ready. Prayers are storming the heavens and binding the "strong men" declaring and decreeing God's Kingdom rule in every jurisdiction. This is what we call Kingdom Advancing Prayer. What a *Glorious Day* to be *Alive* and to be in the *Will* and *Plan of Father God*! *Hallelujah*!

KINGDOM ADVANCING PRAYER VOLUME III

One of the keys to the amazing rise to greater functionality of The Church is the clear understanding of what we call Kingdom Advancing Prayer. This kind of prayer reaches into the very core of the demonic stronghold and destroys demonic kings and princes and establishes the Kingdom and Purpose of the Lord. This is the kind of prayer that Jesus Christ engaged in, to bring to pass the will of His Father while He was upon planet earth.

IDENTIFYING AND DEFEATING THE JEZEBEL SPIRIT

I declare to you with the greatest of conviction that we are living in the days when Malachi 4:5-6 is being fulfilled. Elijah in his day had to confront and deal with a false spiritual order and government that was established and set up by an evil woman called Jezebel and her spineless husband called Ahab. This spirit is still active in the earth and in The Church; however the Lord is restoring His holy Apostles and Prophets to identify and destroy this spirit as recorded in Revelation 2:18-23.